Embracing Greatness

A Guide for Living the Life You Love

Sophia Ellen Falke

Embracing Greatness:
A Guide for Living the Life You Love

~ by Sophia Ellen Falke
www.EmbracingGreatness.com
Copyright © 2017

Sojourn Publishing, LLC

ISBN 978-1-62747-067-4 (Paperback)
ISBN 978-1-62747-068-1 (Ebook)

Printed in the United States of America

DEDICATION

To Anna and Ernest Falke, my parents, who gave me life and a foundation.

To Divine Source, God, with which all things are possible.

To Mary Benson and Jim Sherman, my BFFs.

To Mr. Young, my High School guidance counselor, who changed my life.

To everyone who has loved me, hurt me or didn't care, I am grateful. You have been my teachers and guides. Without you, I would not be the person I am today.

And to you, Beloved Seeker, who is reading this book because you are ready to heal old wounds, claim your inner beauty, and radiate your greatness to bless our world.

TABLE OF CONTENTS

FOREWORD

Imagine yourself living the life of your dreams. What would that look like? How would you feel? There are many people for whom living a dream life is a foreign concept. In fact, many are not able to answer the question, "What would you love?"

I've been teaching people to become dream builders and guiding them to living the life they love for over 40 years. It's rewarding and inspiring to witness the transformations people experience when they dare to dream, receive support, and take action in ways that allow their dreams to come true. Often a dream builder will then inspire others to create and live the lives they love, as well.

There are many great teachers and writers who offer inspiration, guidance, and tools for living the life you love. Sophia Falke has been teaching transformation principles for over fifteen years as a speaker, through classes and seminars, and via magazine and newspaper articles. I'm delighted to welcome Sophia to the family of book authors dedicated to guiding and supporting you in demonstrating your unique gifts and passion in the world.

Sophia focuses on several basic principles in *Embracing Greatness: A Guide for Living the Life You Love*:

- You have greatness within you,
- You have a unique gift and purpose to demonstrate in this lifetime,
- It's never too late to create and live the life you would love – a life filled with purpose, fun, and abundance,
- You already have all that you need within you to discover the "how" to live the life you would love.

As you explore *Embracing Greatness*, you'll embark on a journey of self-discovery, empowerment, and transformation. Sophia's book helps you discern the values that guide your life, explains the stages of awakening, offers tools to uncover your dream, and provides foundational and advanced tools for living your dream full out.

Some transformational books focus more on inspiration or theory. And you'll find some of this also in *Embracing Greatness*. However, Sophia includes reflective and practical, hands-on exercises in each chapter that give you a structure for uncovering closely held beliefs and fears that might be holding you back, as well as limiting self-doubts and judgments. She also introduces you to powerful transformational tools such as gratitude, forgiveness, and meditation. And Sophia provides a proven formula for success that she's developed and shared with others to apply in their personal and business lives.

Underlying the principles Sophia presents in *Embracing Greatness* is a spiritual grounding that there is a higher power and order of being that empowers you to live the life of your dreams in full, if you apply the art and science of transformation. Her book also includes the recognition that there is more than enough abundance in the universe that is available to you once you identify, commit to, and become an exact match for what you would love. Sophia shares her own story and the stories of people she has known to demonstrate how you too can live a happier, more expansive, and abundant life.

I first met Sophia almost fifteen years ago when I presented a seminar to the Eastern Region of Unity Churches. We reconnected four years ago when Sophia began offering my Prosperity Plus programs to her Unity church in Las Vegas. She then added to her already substantial teaching and coaching credentials by becoming credentialed in my DreamBuilder® and Life Mastery programs and participating in my accelerated Alpha Omega and Brave Thinking® Masters programs. So, I've now known Sophia Falke as a colleague, student, and friend and have seen her true heart, abundance consciousness, and dedication to creating a better world.

Throughout her life, Sophia has demonstrated that it's never too late to create and live the life you love as she continues to follow her passion and spread her message of love and firm belief in the inherent greatness in everyone. If you're ready to live the life you would love, and willing to take the life-empowering steps toward your dream, then *Embracing Greatness: A Guide for Living the Life You Love* is for you. You will forever thank yourself for reading and applying this wonderful book.

Mary Morrissey
International Speaker, Best-Selling Author,
CEO Consultant, Visionary, Empowerment Specialist

PREFACE

"GREATNESS:
An internal calling which speaks so powerfully that you
experience all the peace, love, joy, and abundance
necessary to live the life you love."
– Sophia Falke

Why *Embracing Greatness*?

Over the many years I've walked this beautiful earth, I've discovered that one of our major human challenges is we continuously suppress the spark of greatness each of us has within. Our conditioning is to be modest, humble, and self-effacing. Yet the Biblical creation story teaches you are made in the image and likeness of God. This means you have a divinity and greatness within you. The message is you're co-creators with God and, as such, are obligated to demonstrate the essence of God that you are.

Greatness is inherent in each of us. Yet we hold back for various reasons. We're taught it's arrogant to excel if it could make others look less competent, attractive, or desirable. There's a family to raise. Someone needs caregiving. Or you experienced financial, emotional, or physical setbacks. The list is endless – but that was then.

This is now. And *now* is your time. It's your time to express the greatness that lies in your soul.

I wrote *Embracing Greatness* because I believe there is a curiosity and yearning in each of us that's crying out to be revealed. Author Tom Bird says that books are already written in the spiritual realm but have no substance in the physical world until you write them. So if I believe I'm co-creating with God (and I do), it's time I did my part. And I have friends who tell me what I have to say needs to be shared. Nothing in *Embracing Greatness* is new. There are many teachers and books I've learned from and been inspired by. However, as my friends point out, these principles haven't been expressed with my voice.

In addition, I believe I must do several things if I am to help others. First, I can only guide you to the level that I have been willing to work toward achieving. Writing this book is part of my own spiritual journey and inner soul work. Second, completing this book throws open energetic gates to more greatness in my own life. And third, this book enables me to serve people I may never meet, but about whom I care deeply. My personal vision is to transform the world. I can do this – one thought, one word, and one action at a time. This book is a physical demonstration of that vision.

I'm publishing *Embracing Greatness* as I complete seventy turns around the sun. It has been, and continues to be, a full life – one in which I've repeatedly discovered that every moment is an opportunity to embrace my own greatness and support others in embracing – and demonstrating – theirs. My desire is that after reading *Embracing Greatness*, you'll discover that your time is *now*, no matter how young or old you are, how "smart" or "average," how "accomplished" or "challenged," or what your life circumstances are today. Whatever your history (or herstory), remember, this is how your life has been "up until now." And *now* is when you're claiming your true nature and recognizing it's time to embrace your greatness.

It doesn't matter what your circumstances were "up until now." Whether you're a busboy, housewife, executive, retiree, college grad, high school dropout, ex-con, entertainer, living on the streets, or president of the United States, there is still more greatness within you yearning to be revealed and celebrated in the world. I've written *Embracing Greatness* for you. You're reading it because you recognize there's still something for you to do – you just might not be sure yet what that is or how to accomplish it.

Your greatness already exists in the spiritual realm. Now it's up to you, if you so choose, to give it body here in the physical world. Return your attention to the Biblical creation stories, remembering you are made in the image and likeness of God and given dominion over all that God created. With that pedigree, how could you be anything less than great? In fact, you and I have a sacred honor and responsibility to demonstrate God (Creator, Source) in all its splendor and glory in the world.

As you look around you, you'll notice many worn and weary people who are filling roles in life for which they have no passion – like actors in a play who have walk-on parts, yet have a yearning and passion in their hearts to be the star. They've accepted parts that don't fit with their heart's desire and followed other people's dreams instead of their own. Or could that be you? I know I've faced some of this myself. Stereotypical labels, expectations, and limitations can be stifling. Sometimes I acquiesced to them; other times I danced to my own inner music. What's *your* music? What's the starring role in life that *you* are meant to play?

Thank you for allowing me to support you and be part of your journey. I feel blessed to be invited into your life as you read *Embracing Greatness: A Guide for Living the Life You Love* and incorporate these principles into your life.

Sophia

INTRODUCTION

"The only value we have as human beings
is the risks we're willing to take."
– Ernest Hemmingway

ALASKA

"You must be the Alaska daughter," the elder ladies of my mother's church said as, one by one, they gently reached out and touched my arm. It was my mother's funeral service. I was "the Alaska daughter" because two years earlier, I had taken my mother on a 10,000-mile camping adventure from my home in Tucson, Arizona, to the Arctic Circle north of Fairbanks, Alaska.

It was 1989 and, at seventy-five, it was Mom's first camping trip. I almost didn't invite her, wondering if she would be comfortable on a two-and-a-half-month trek with few of the amenities of home. I was driving my three-quarter-ton pickup truck that had a fully self-contained camper held securely in the truck bed. That meant we had a three-burner stove, a small refrigerator, heat, comfortable beds, and, most importantly, a toilet and large water tank. (If you've ever driven in Alaska, you know that having these basics is essential for your comfort.) But would that be enough?

At first, Mom was nervous. Early in our trip, she asked that we leave a particular campground before settling in because she didn't feel "right" there. It meant that I drove two more hours to another camping area, but I happily did so because I had promised Mom we would leave any place where she didn't feel safe, no questions asked. It was important to me that my mother feel secure and have a positive once-in-a-lifetime experience.

Another request Mom made was for full hookups (electric, sewer, water). But as we explored the amazing wonders of the western United States and Canada, she started looking in the campground books for remote, rustic campsites where the sky was so clear the stars would come down to kiss us good night each evening. We followed in the steps of ancient people, walked on glaciers thousands of years old, looked into the eyes of aging totems, fished for salmon on the Kenai Peninsula, met caribou and moose, badger and bear, and beheld beauty that took our breath away.

Most precious was our time together. We joked that I did the "manly man" duties of driving, general maintenance, and, most elegant of all, emptying the refuse tanks at dump stations. Mom handled the "womanly woman" tasks of cooking and washing dishes. Other duties were shared, but our most important sharing was our love and joy of being together and creating beautiful memories to last a lifetime. For Mom, that lifetime was two more years. For me, the memories still live in my heart. I recall especially standing with my mother on a bridge over the Yukon River as we shared a priceless experience of watching a brilliant, shimmering sun sink over the western horizon, setting the river on fire with a cacophony of crimsons and golds.

Throughout this book, I'll refer to my Alaska experience. We all have special stories and memories that were pivotal in making us the unique expressions of the higher order of being that we are today. Some experiences we label "good," others as "bad." Which definition you choose depends on the lenses, or filters, through which you view life's events and conditions. Our experiences, and how we define them, make you and me who we are today – either as powerful, ever-expanding creators of lives worth living or as negative, constricting, destructive forces.

There's a back story to the Alaska adventure with my mother. It was an emotionally painful period; however, it was the catalyst to living the life I would love.

The story begins when I was in the throes of misery and uncertainty in my job at a Tucson hospital. I went to see a trusted advisor to share how desolate I was feeling and to seek some outside advice. I allowed myself to be vulnerable and gave a tearful rendition of my situation. He listened quietly, letting me share until I had spent my built-up feelings of helplessness and fear. When I had finished, he paused and said, "I think it's important for people to come to their own decisions, so I don't usually offer direct advice. But in your case, I'm making an exception. I think you should leave your job."

Leave my job? My mind started to reel. My first thoughts were, "How can I leave? I don't have any prospects. I haven't even thought of finding another job." I'm sure my face telegraphed the mental mischief that had erupted from his suggestion.

He pulled a single sheet of paper from a file drawer and gave me this quote by W. H. Murray of the Scottish Himalayan Expedition, which said,

> *"Until one is committed there is hesitancy, the chance to draw back, always ineffectiveness. Concerning all acts of initiative (and creation) there is one elementary truth, the ignorance of which kills countless ideas and splendid plans: that the moment one definitely commits oneself, then Providence moves too. All sorts of things occur to help one that would never otherwise have occurred.*

A whole stream of events issues from the decision,
raising in one's favour all manner of unforeseen
incidents and meetings and material assistance,
which no man could have dreamt would have come
his way. I have learned a deep respect for one of
Goethe's couplets:

'Whatever you can do, or dream you can, begin it.
Boldness has genius, power and magic in it."

I felt chills when I read it. Yes, the thought of leaving my job felt scary. It also felt right, and I said, "That's a huge decision. I'll have to sleep on it." And that was my intention. Go home, maybe call a few friends for advice, and sleep on it. It was 5:00 pm, so I decided to go home. But the next thing I knew I was at the hospital and, finding my boss still in his office, gave three months' notice. Three months would take me to my fifth anniversary. Plus, I probably thought I'd have a plan B in place by then. One thing I knew for sure as I left my boss's office: I didn't have a clue what I would do after leaving the hospital.

On the way home, I remembered the W. H. Murray quote. "Until one is committed..." Oh drat, I have nothing to commit to. What to do? I think it was about the first time I ever asked myself, "What would I truly love?" At this point in my life, I had accomplished a fair amount professionally, mostly because my career or educational moves were made from the position of discontent with what I was doing and a desire for something more. But "What would I love?" I don't think I had really asked myself that question. Certainly, no one else had asked me.

What would I love? I thought about that for a few days. What did I enjoy doing in general? I enjoyed traveling, seeing new scenery and architecture, and experiencing different cultures. Yes, I would travel. Okay, where? I had just attended a presentation by a woman who had spent a year in the Alaska wilderness with her fiancé and a dog. They had built their own log cabin; killed, butchered, and preserved a moose for the winter months; and endured a long, harsh winter. The wilderness log cabin, moose butchering, and hard winter didn't appeal to me, but the thought of visiting Alaska – in the summer – did. I read James Michener's novel *Alaska*. That solidified my desire. I fell in love with the history; the rugged natural beauty; the people, totems, and glaciers – and the spirit of our 49th state.

I thought it would be amazing to drive all the way to Prudhoe Bay; but at the time, private vehicles weren't allowed that far north on the haul road that ran along the

Alaska pipeline. I could, however, easily reach the Arctic Circle. I'm not sure why, but that desire took hold.

"Until one is committed..." I now had my vision – The Arctic Circle in Alaska. I didn't know how I would do that. However, as I was to discover, the strength and passion that was growing in my heart and mind would take care of the "how."

I shared my dream with friends and co-workers. My secretary sent for information from the Alaska tourist bureau. I ordered *The Alaska Milepost*, a book that described just about everything along most of Alaska's highways and byways. Slowly a plan emerged. I would camp my way from Tucson, Arizona, to the Arctic Circle in Alaska.

I realized that if I went on this adventure, I wouldn't be able to support my house payments. I decided to sell my home. I also realized my little Toyota Corolla wasn't the vehicle for such an arduous trip. I didn't know what was, just that the Corolla wasn't. So I put my house on the market and started car shopping. Finding the right vehicle was a challenge, since I didn't know what I wanted. I advertised my car, not realizing it would sell immediately. Now I had no car. But I was certainly committing.

Here's where the next part of the Murray quotation came into play; namely, that "...all manner of unforeseen" resources and circumstances came my way. Friends loaned me their automobiles while I looked for my Alaska vehicle. I discovered it's like taking a walk up a hill. You know your destination lies on the other side, but you can't see it yet. With every step, all you can see is the path in front of you. But you know that your goal is "just on the other side." And then you take the crucial next step that makes it possible for you to see over the hilltop. And there it is! You can see your destination. A step before, it was still out of view. But now you can see it. That's exactly how my process unfolded.

I finally decided to purchase a three-quarter-ton GMC pickup and a camper to put in the truck bed. I went through a broker for the truck and purchased a used camper from a private seller. As with selling my car before getting the replacement vehicle, I did things backward again. I took possession of the camper before I received delivery of the truck. Because I had already sold my home, I had no place to put the camper. A friend offered her side yard, so I had the camper delivered there and moved in.

Before the house sold, my mother came for a visit. I hadn't told her about quitting my job, putting the house up for sale, or planning to drive to Alaska. As I drove Mom home from the airport, I said, "Mom, there's something I haven't told you. There's a 'For Sale' sign in my front yard." That caught her attention, and she looked over at me. "And there's more," I said. "I quit my job." That really got her attention. "Oh, did you find something new?" she asked. "No Mom, I have nothing in the wings." She started to speak up. And I knew what she would say. "How can you leave a job when you don't have another? What do you mean you're selling your house? Where will you live?" I knew what she would say, because these were the paradigms she was raised with and had infused in me.

I also knew how to keep the conversation from taking that turn. Mom loved to travel. I used to joke that all I'd have to say is, "Mom, would you like to go to X?" and she'd be standing by the door, bags packed, asking, "What's taking you so long?"

So I quickly said, "I've decided to go on a camping trip to Alaska. Would you like to come?" That stopped her in her tracks. Alaska? New adventure? Yes, I knew how to get my mother's attention. Now my dream had expanded. It included someone very special to me, someone who would share that dream 100 percent.

I was just walking up that hill. One step at a time.

I released most of my possessions, put the rest into storage, took possession of my camper, then my truck. And we had fun, even before we left. Again, the dream was so solid, so vivid, so magnetic, that all my friends, and even strangers, started living the dream with me. We explored the RV stores, pored over the books I had gathered, and mapped out our trip.

There were some hiccups along the way, conditions such as the Arizona Department of Motor Vehicles confiscating my truck title from the broker I used when he went bankrupt, which made it impossible to get license plates in time for my departure. But, ahh, the power of a clear dream. The agent at DMV caught my dream and took extraordinary measures to make sure I had all the paperwork I needed to go on my adventure. I noticed that some of the people who helped me attain my dream only came into my life long enough to help me with one small part of the journey. For example, a car salesman helped me hone my understanding of what vehicle would best serve me and then was gone. The DMV clerk performed one, very essential, function to keep me on course. I never saw her again.

I'm grateful for these special people. We all have them. They help us complete our journeys. Our lives are an invitation to recognize and appreciate their contributions to us, as well as how we impact others, and how we are all united as one.

Of course, there's more to this story. However, I wanted to give you a taste of how discovering your answer to the question, "What would I love?" will help you create a life worth living and experiences worth treasuring. That means creating a clear vision, infusing it with the power of your passion, and taking action in response to the pull of your dream.

Chapter I

WHAT KEEPS YOU FROM LIVING LIFE "FULL OUT"?

"You are the light of the world. A city set on a hill cannot be hidden; nor does anyone light a lamp and put it under a basket, but on the lampstand, and it gives light to all who are in the house. "Let your light shine before men in such a way that they may see your good works, and glorify your Father who is in heaven."
– Matthew 5:14-16

"Don't die with your music still in you."
– Wayne Dyer

Mattie had a passion for helping others. After a lifetime of betrayals, including her husband pimping her out to other men so he could watch from the shadows, and then later trying to steal her children, Mattie fought back and rose above these challenging outer conditions. My heart swelled with admiration and compassion as I learned of her hardships and overcoming.

She said, "I've got a story to tell. I've had so many trials in my life, I want to write a book so that young people going

1

through abuse can see there's hope and a better life waiting." This candid statement came ten minutes into my conversation with Mattie, a thin, stand-tall 72-year-old woman living in rural Arkansas. We met at a hospice memorial service led by a colleague of mine. Mattie was a volunteer, dedicated to helping others, wanting to help even more. Fortunately, her desire to help was stronger than her Arkansas pride that told her she had to figure everything out on her own. We began a long, fruitful relationship as I coached her from "I want to write" to "I just published my book."

Mattie is "Everywoman," "Everyman." There was a greatness in her yearning to break free. Mattie was fortunate. At least she knew what she wanted to do – share her story to lessen others' suffering and show people a way out. Life could be better. She had learned that life is a grand adventure to be savored, celebrated, and shared.

Sadly, many people aren't in touch with their inner flame that's ready and waiting to be ignited. Perhaps you're reading this book because you're one of them, smothering your flame under a lifetime of should, gotta, can't, and plain old ignorance that there is a better way. Perhaps you're reading because you're doing well but are experiencing a growing discontent and hearing an inner voice telling you there's something better for you.

There are many reasons we hide our light, or at least dim it. Those around us who are afraid to live life to the fullest often try to hold us back so that they don't have to look at their own fears and insecurities. In the Sermon on the Mount, Jesus admonished us not to hide our light under a bushel. Instead, put it on a lampstand and let it shine for all to see. That's what it means to be great. Let your light shine. Uncover all your talents and potential. Expand and build on them. Share them as a shining example for others to follow as they too own their potential and promise. And celebrate the fullness and greatness of who you truly are. It's your time – and that time is now.

Ah, but there be pirates and whirlpools and dragons out there – obstacles that hold you back. They have many names, and name them we must, because in the awareness of life's demons, the journey to overcoming and thriving begins.

Living on Autopilot

"Oh God, is it Monday… already?" I'd groan as I stuck my foot out from under the warmth of my down comforter onto the cold, wooden floor of my Boston apartment. I'd stumble through my shower, brush my teeth, and push myself out the door every morning, walking briskly to the

Orange Line and wedging my body into a crowded train with hundreds of other commuters. I'd transfer to the Blue Line, get off at Government Center, jaywalk to my building, grab a coffee and muffin from the snack shop, and take the elevator to the tenth floor and another humdrum day of sameness and repetition at an average job that required little imagination or creativity.

Sound familiar? You drag yourself out of bed each morning. Grab the same breakfast. Follow the same route to work. Participate in the same conversations with co-workers you have every Monday morning as you enter into the same routine. Oh, no, another week of "same ol', same ol'," another week of drudgery.

Or perhaps your "same ol'" means preparing the same lesson plans for school, cooking the same meals for your family, making the same sales calls, leading the same team of corporate vice presidents, seeing the same patients, handling the same customer questions, driving the same route, and doing the same things over and over again. Perhaps at one time you were excited about and loved your life. But now you've been following the same routine for so long, the bloom is off the rose. The excitement and newness you once felt are long since over. In fact, you've done the "same ol' thing" so many times, you could almost do it in your sleep. You're doing it for the paycheck, and that's it. You feel like you're on autopilot for a life of sameness and drudgery.

Autopilot "doing" begins with autopilot thinking and repeatedly responding to outside conditions the same ol' way again and again. Autopilot thinking could look like:

- The Dow dips? "Ack! The economy is crashing."
- People are losing their jobs? "I'll probably be next."
- Diagnosed with cancer? "I'm going to die."
- A relationship breaks up? "I'll never find another love."
- Stuck in traffic? "That guy's out to get me."

Autopilot isn't just about negative, knee-jerk responses. You might also be so worn down by circumstances that you put a happy face on everything – even when it's unhealthy for you physically, mentally, or spiritually. "That's just the way things are" might be your mantra.

- Your boss constantly criticizes your work. You think, "She's trying to help me improve."
- Your spouse always blames you or anyone other than himself for having a bad day. You think, "He's a sensitive man. He needs my understanding."

- Your alcoholic parent puts you down again and again. You think, "I know they love me. That must be what love looks like."

When you find yourself in the autopilot cycle, it means you've given up control of your life. You've gone unconscious without even realizing it. I can relate. My autopilot life included many good co-workers and friends, and a lot of great times. My autopilot thinking went everywhere with me. When I left a job and moved to more challenging work, autopilot was there. When I began a new relationship, autopilot went on every date with me. When I celebrated another birthday, autopilot helped me blow out the candles on the birthday cake. Bottom line, you can be on autopilot whether you're clerking, herding cattle, cleaning floors, teaching, parenting, building skyscrapers, or leading a Fortune 500 company.

If you recognize yourself living a life on autopilot, take heart. *Embracing Greatness* offers tools to break free of autopilot and actually create a life you love. I did it, I've helped many others do it, and I'm 100 percent confident you can do it too.

Letting Life "Should" On You

Have you ever been "should upon"? That's when your family, school, employers, or society in general tells you what you "should" or "should not" do. Yes, it's not wise to put your hand into a roaring fire. So some "shoulds" are appropriate. But then there are shoulds that are based on "how things have always been done" or what's comfortable for others. I know I was "should upon" for many years. In the 1960s, the "shoulds" for girls and women were strict. They included "You should find a man, get married, and raise a family." It was okay to get a job initially after graduating high school or technical college. But once married, you had children and stayed home until they went off to school. The job you accepted had to be gender appropriate, meaning secretarial, teaching or nursing, and within the confines of what women "should do." If you remained single, you were a spinster or an old maid and a failure.

The "shoulds" upon men were similarly restrictive. You were expected to get married and have children. It was your job to bear the full responsibility of supporting your family, even if it meant holding down two or three jobs. You didn't show emotion and were expected to always be strong. You fought for your country and were expected to step back into civilian life – to be a loving father, son, spouse – as if you had never experienced the horrors of war.

All of us were expected to adhere to the rules for our gender, whether we liked them or not.

Times have changed, but "shoulds" are still firmly in place. Women and men have made great strides in shedding their inflexible gender roles. However, there are different shoulds in today's world. In addition to gender, we face pressure to look a certain way no matter what our age, thanks to Madison Avenue and airbrushing. You "should" have a bigger home, live in a more upscale, eco-friendly community, be "seen" with the right people, or have the latest, and the coolest, new technology.

The "shoulds" start with your family, ethnic or racial group, and religion. You might have been "should upon" by the children you played with, your school, how "smart" people said you were, and what clubs or athletic activities you were encouraged or allowed to participate in. Society, higher learning, and your employers "should" on top of the many layers of "should" that already restricted you and kept you separated from what you really wanted in your life.

Your "shoulds" might also include:

- sexual orientation
- the color of your skin
- how talented or smart you are (or people think you are)
- what part of the country or world you come from
- your politics
- your profession
- if you're thin or fat, tall or short
- even your hair color ("blond" joke anyone?)

Then there are the "shoulds" of how you should think, how you should judge people and situations, how you should know your place, and even how you should leave this world. The list is endless. Is it any wonder you might be struggling under the yoke of so much "should" weight? And isn't it time to shed that weight?

"But I've Always Done It This Way."

Want to kill innovation and the excitement of discovery? Just say "I've always done it this way." I heard those words a lot when I worked at a government office. No one seemed to know why they followed certain procedures, just that it had "always been that way." At first,

I thought I was the only one bothered by these explanations. I know my questions bothered some of the long-time employees. Later, when the Governor introduced a quality improvement initiative that required us to ask a lot of "why" questions, I discovered that many of my co-workers were as frustrated as I was with the "we've always done it that way" explanations.

I became chief of the office of quality support and training for my department when I worked for the State of Arizona. One of the stories I used when I trained teams was about a newlywed who cut off the end of a roast before putting it in the roasting pan. Her husband asked, "Why are you doing that? There's plenty of room in the pan." She replied, "My mother always did it this way." Later she told the story to her mother and asked, "Why do you cut off the end of the roast?" Her mother answered, "Because my mother always did it that way." So they decided to ask Grandma, who laughed when she discovered she had unintentionally started a tradition. "I cut the end off," Grandma answered, "because my oven was too small for a large roasting pan."

In the case of the government office, "I've always done it this way" led to inefficiencies, stagnation, cost overruns, customer dissatisfaction, and low morale. Eliminating that statement from our government vocabulary led to many innovations and brought a fresh sense of expectation and excitement among many government employees. Asking "Why?" wasn't always easy for some. However, it was the only way to refresh and rejuvenate government services.

The "I've always done it this way" syndrome is also present in the private and non-profit sectors. Those that don't continuously ask themselves "Why?" or keep their finger on the pulse of their particular industries will be left behind in an ever-changing, ever-evolving world that is experiencing innovation and creativity faster, and at exponentially higher levels, than ever before.

I've seen this happen in the United States, impacting entire industries. As coal has been replaced by natural gas, solar, and other energy sources, entire communities have been devastated. People lost their livelihoods, and no one addressed what other opportunities could be created for them. Years ago companies decided to "flatten" their organizational structures and thousands of middle managers found themselves jobless. Automation and outsourcing to other countries have eliminated countless manufacturing jobs. Many of the people impacted languished because they allowed outer conditions to dictate the quality of their lives.

On an individual level, you'll discover that relying on how you've always done something without periodically shining a fresh light on it and asking "Why?" will hold you back from doing and being your best self. "I've always done it that way" creates a breeding ground for crisis situations that show up later in life as health challenges, relationship issues, job disruptions, or simply general boredom and malaise.

F.E.A.R.

Fear: "An unpleasant emotion caused by the belief that someone or something is dangerous, likely to cause pain, or a threat." Or at least that's what a dictionary definition will say. But to scientists, the definition isn't quite as clear. While the physiological effects of fear are generally recognized, the neural pathways and connections that cause these effects are not as well understood. From the evolutionary standpoint, the theory is that fear is a neural circuit that has been designed to keep an organism alive in dangerous situations.

How does it work? Learning and responding to stimuli that warn of danger involve neural pathways sending information about the outside world to the amygdala (an almond-shaped mass of cells within the temporal lobe of the brain), which determines the significance of the stimulus and triggers emotional responses like flight or fight.

Our caveman ancestors stood at the mouth of their cave and assessed any danger that might lurk outside the cave entrance. They needed to be afraid. There were many ferocious animals outside the safety of their cave that were faster, meaner, bigger, and better equipped with claws and fangs for killing.

We aren't cavemen anymore (at least most of us aren't). True, there are still parts of the world where people have to be on high alert due to gangs, terrorists, rogue bands of rebel forces, or even dangerous animals. Our military forces in combat zones must also be ever vigilant. However, in most of the world, we no longer have to function continuously in danger mode. In fact, operating at this level unnecessarily stresses our bodies and consciousness and often leads to physical and mental illness.

Fear can be a healthy early-warning sign to keep you safe. Or it can be a debilitating, defeating, dysfunctional drain on your energy and life purpose. Yet you might believe your fears and false perceptions are real. Sometimes you use them as justification for avoiding personal and professional growth. Or you might have been taught to be afraid of the unknown, of people different from you, or of challenging situations.

The acronym for fear is False Evidence Appearing Real. My "false evidence" showed up when I was afraid to leave a particular job, even though I hated going to work every day. "What's the worst that could happen if you left your job?" a friend asked me. "I wouldn't be able to find another job," I answered. "What's the worst that could happen if you couldn't find another job?" he asked. "I wouldn't have money to pay my mortgage," I responded. "What's the worst that could happen if you couldn't pay your mortgage?"

He continued asking the same question, "What's the worst that could happen if …" over and over until I realized remaining in a job I hated was worse than any "what if" repercussions. It became clear to me I didn't have anything to fear and I was greater than the outer conditions I was facing. With the new awareness, I even began asking myself, "Is there something wonderful that could happen if I left my job?"

My mother used to express her concern when I shared my thoughts about embarking on some new venture. For years, I allowed her anxiety to cloud my own self-confidence. Eventually, I realized I was letting my mother's fears hold me back. Mom still shared her apprehensions, but instead of accepting them as my own, I started responding with, "Thanks, Mom, for your concern. I think I'll let you worry. That way I won't have to." And I didn't.

Studies indicate that most people are more afraid of public speaking than of dying. I don't know if I fall into this category, but I do remember hating having to speak or present in public. Plus, I know I was pretty awful and could have easily won the "Queen of Monotone" crown. Then I discovered a small Toastmasters International group. At the first meeting, I witnessed a man who had the worst grammar I had ever encountered mesmerize me with his story. He simply showed up as his natural self. It was then I realized that public speaking was not putting on some false persona. It was simply being myself and honing my presentation skills. Now I enjoy public speaking and do it every week.

When you feel fearful, yes, do a check-in to see if there is any basis for fear. Usually, the answer is "no." Even if it is "yes," it might be time to feel the fear and take action anyway. The amazing thing about this process is that once you do whatever you were afraid of, you find there was probably nothing to be afraid of, and you expand your comfort zone to the point that it's no longer frightening. In fact, the new (and previously frightening) experience is now your normalcy.

Obstacles: Don't Think You Have the Talent, Resources & Support You Need?

When you come down to it, most of the obstacles we encounter are those we self-impose because of our beliefs and attitudes. Henry Ford said, "If you think you can do something or if you think you can't do something, you're right." So if you think you don't have the talent, resources or support you need, you're right. But if you think you do, you're also right.

"But I don't have the knowledge I need to reach my dream," you might be thinking. Again, it's what you believe that's important. Today the excuse "lack of knowledge" holds water like a sieve. We now have the Internet, which has search engines, chat rooms, instructional videos, encyclopedias, dictionaries, expert websites, Facebook, LinkedIn, and more. There are people already doing what you want to do, and many of them would be happy to mentor you. Whether you learn best visually, orally, or experientially, the resources are available. There are also people with whom you can partner. Steven Spielberg doesn't know how to do everything that goes into making a movie. He does know how to engage the people who have the talents he needs. Just look at the hundreds of credits that follow every film.

You don't have to know *how* to do everything. You *do* need to become clear in your vision and reach out to those who have the skills you require.

I enjoy the stories about some of the tech world stars such as Mark Zuckerberg, who dropped out of Harvard in his sophomore year to start Facebook, and Bill Gates, who also dropped out of Harvard to start Microsoft. Yes, both were brilliant in their fields. But they could have gone the way of many brilliant programmers of their day and gotten "real jobs" and followed a traditional path of "shoulds." Instead, they became trailblazers, reshaping the world as we know it.

Want an example with humbler beginnings than the Zuckerbergs and Gateses of the world? They're all around you. We've all known them. It might be your neighbor, a colleague, or someone you met while standing in line at the grocery store. That successful, confident woman might have been a single mom with little education who'd had enough of putting her children to bed hungry, wondering if she could make the rent, and lamenting that she had no future. Or that poised, self-assured man in line ahead of you could be a man who was abused as a child, had buried himself in drugs and alcohol, and had lost all hope. Yet they got angry enough – or had a strong enough yearning for a better life – and began their journey back from despair.

They encountered naysayers on their journeys, as will you. But naysayers cannot stop you when your dream is clear enough, strong enough, and passionate enough to draw you to it, giving you the necessary resources to overcome outer limitations and conditions.

You may encounter resistance, indifference, or hostility when you attempt to make a change. Family, friends, or co-workers might not support you in living the life you love. The opposition can be subtle, even insidious. How do you persevere? In the following chapters, I offer you effective tools to help you transcend others' attempts to limit you in living the life you would love. These tools will help you create "yesses" that are greater than others' "nos."

Don't Have the Money?

I could easily have put money in the sections about fear or obstacles. However, money has such a strong charge for many of us that it deserves its own conversation.

If you want to see people twitch, mention money. Many of us are taught early in life that it's impolite or impolitic to talk about money. Many churches misinterpret or misquote scripture and say that money is the root of all evil. The truth is, money is a form of energy or exchange. Nothing more. Nothing less. Yet you may base important life decisions on an elevated sense of the importance of money. Yes, money – as a form of energy or exchange – needs to be part of many decisions. Too many people in this country are in serious credit card debt because they don't have a healthy relationship with money. For them, money has become a minor deity, at whose altar they worship. It's not the money. It's your relationship with money.

I remember a time when the only things in my purse related to money were cash and a checkbook. If I didn't have it, I didn't spend it. Today I have multiple debit and credit cards, some offering me miles for every dollar I charge, or cash back at the end of the year. This shift to a credit-based society has changed our relationship with money. And it has created an unconscious, zombie state when it comes to good stewardship of our financial resources.

In 2000 I attended a workshop led by Dr. Maria Nemeth, author of *The Energy of Money* and founder of The Academy for Coaching Excellence. Our homework before we came to the first session was to find out how much money we had – to the penny. That included money in the bank, investments, and retirement funds. One by one she called us forward and asked us to share with the entire group the amount of money we had. It was truly an invitation to becoming conscious.

In her book, Dr. Nemeth says, "Our relationship with money is a metaphor for our relationship with all forms of energy: time, physical vitality, enjoyment, creativity, and the support of friends." So money isn't just about money. If you take money for granted, are there other areas of your life – like your relationships – that you take for granted? Do you waste the money you have? If so, do you find you're also wasting a lot of your time?

Take time to uncover your relationship with money. You can start by determining how much money you actually have available from all channels. What is your debt? If your debt is greater than your current financial resources, what emotions and beliefs about yourself come up? Breathe. This is the time to be truthful with yourself so that you become conscious. Telling the truth and being an objective observer (no judgment), opens up breathing space so that you can take authentic action regarding your finances.

We live in an abundant universe. The main thing that prevents you and me from claiming that abundance is our own mental mischief that says, "Life is hard," "There isn't enough," "It's wrong to be wealthy," or "People like me just don't get the breaks." You can probably add to this list.

Are you ready to release your doubts and fears so you can reach your dream? Are you ready to live the life you love? If you are, keep reading. It's your choice.

Chapter II
RECOGNITION

*"Beneath the apparent circumstances of
every situation exists a wholly different
reality – a different world altogether."*
– Colin Tipping

*"Greatness is something that's in you right now, in a way
as unique as your fingerprint and soulprint. Great moments
can happen spontaneously at any time, like a moment when
you see a flower and you don't just walk by; you take a
moment to appreciate it, and to see the whole universe
alive in that opening bloom."*
– Mary Morrissey

"This Ain't It."

In the 1960s, singer Peggy Lee regaled listeners with a
song that asked, "Is that all there is?" It's a question that
even the most affluent, famous, and successful people often
ask. It's a question that tells us something is missing,
regardless of outer displays of wealth and achievement. It's
a discontent that arises because in your heart you know

there's something bigger and better for you. You just don't know what it is yet. Another way to say it is that you don't know what you don't know. But the discontent, the "Is that all there is?" yearning is calling you higher.

Don't Know What You Don't Know

I would ask you what you don't know, except it's an impossible question to answer. If you don't know you don't know, then you are living in not-so-blissful ignorance. This is possibly the most difficult mindset to penetrate. Before Columbus discovered America, except for the Vikings, few Europeans knew there was any land west of Portugal. They didn't know what they didn't know. It took a Columbus to know what he didn't know to discover America.

Imagine what it was like for the native population of the Bahamas when the first European ships came into sight. Were they even able to see the ships, because a floating vessel of that size was totally outside their awareness? Or consider what it would be like for someone who has never seen an airplane, trying to explain a propeller that spins so fast it looks like a solid disc. As long as the propeller continues turning at full speed, there would be no way to convince someone who had never seen such a phenomenon that the solid disc he saw was actually two blades spinning at 1500 rpm.

There are four stages of awareness:

- The first stage is not knowing what you don't know, or ignorance.
- The second stage is knowing what you don't know. It is here that learning or transformation can begin.
- The third stage is knowing what you know. You have studied to gain a certain level of competence, and you feel confident in your abilities.
- The fourth stage is mastery, where you are so skilled or knowledgeable that a particular expertise or practice is part of your DNA.

You will find you're at all of these stages at all times. For example, someone who has achieved mastery in a spiritual sense may know that she doesn't know how to fly a plane and may choose never to master that ability.

DON'T KNOW WHAT YOU DON'T KNOW Unconscious Incompetence	KNOW WHAT YOU DON'T KNOW Conscious Incompetence
MASTERY Unconscious Competence	KNOW WHAT YOU KNOW Conscious Competence

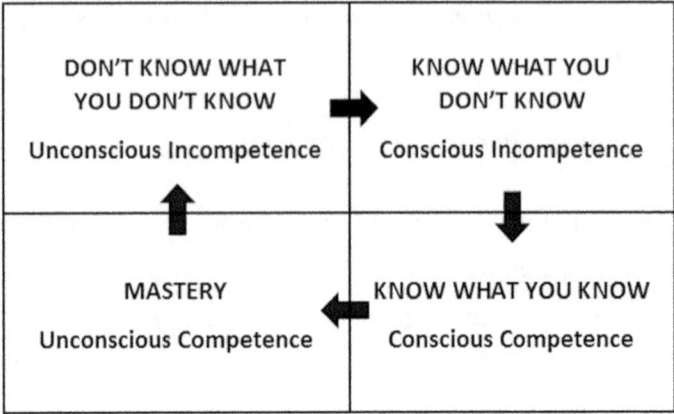

The first stirring of awareness that there might be something you don't know you don't know can be frightening or exhilarating – or both. One thing is for sure, "first contact" with a new paradigm or way of thinking is essential to living a more fulfilling, abundant life.

Obviously, I can't ask you what you don't know you don't know (since you don't know). However, think back and identify areas where you were once totally ignorant about something physical, mental, or spiritual. For example, I didn't know that the thoughts I focus on become my reality. Once I had this new awareness, I knew that I hadn't known that spiritual principle. I decided to pay attention to what I focused on and shift my thinking to expansive thoughts. Slowly I moved toward Mastery. You might not have known that new species of animals are still being discovered. And because you didn't know that you didn't know, it never dawned on you to seek out the information.

Discontent

> *"Healthy discontent is the prelude to progress."*
> – Mahatma Gandhi

> *"Discontent is the first necessity of progress."*
> – Thomas A. Edison

Toby had come to the realization that his work was not what he wanted to do. The energy of being in the wrong job was so strong that he quit. He didn't know what he wanted to do. He had no clue what his purpose and passion were. He just knew that the profession he had been involved in for most of his adult life fell into the category of "This ain't it." It was a profession that paid well and had great stability. He could have found a job anywhere in the United States. But he was unhappy and felt unfulfilled.

I could relate. It's how I had felt years earlier just before I embarked on my Alaska adventure that I described in the Introduction. I too had left my job without knowing what was next. It was the right decision for both Toby and me. We needed to leave our jobs to discover our passion.

Neither of us discovered it right away. Leaving where we were unhappy created the space for us to discover what our unique, individual purpose and passion were.

Other Clues That "This Ain't It"

"Oh, it must be wonderful to be Mary (or Joe, or Harry, or Ethel)." Can you think of people whose lives you find more exciting and interesting than your own? Do you daydream about what it must be like to be them? Do you try to live vicariously through them? You may think you simply appreciate and respect them. Yet by digging deeper, you may discover that your seeming admiration is really discontent with your own life and a desire for "something more."

Or perhaps you constantly put others' needs before your own? You may think it's noble to put others first. After all, you're being of service or a good parent or loving spouse. The truth is, if you put others first most of the time, it might be because you don't think well enough of yourself and your life choices to take care of *you.* So you play second fiddle, not knowing what you want from life.

Other clues that "This ain't it" are physical and mental health challenges. There are many documented stories of people diagnosed with cancer or other debilitating diseases who experience "miraculous" healings when they let go of unhappy marriages, leave dysfunctional relationships, or finally follow their own dreams. I remember being ready to give up my dream of ministry for a relationship. I found myself deferring to his needs and expectations. I believed him when he pointed out my faults and shortcomings and strived to be "better" to win his approval. It took several physical challenges to wake me up to how abusive his behavior was and how dysfunctional our relationship had become. As soon as I ended the relationship, my health problems evaporated.

As a hospital chaplain, then as a coach and spiritual leader, I've met many people who find themselves facing serious mental and physical health challenges that were the result of stress, unhappiness, resentment, or anger. Any one of these emotions can be toxic if held onto. When you cling to two or more, the results can be deadly – physically, spiritually, emotionally, and relationally.

Perhaps you lack energy, find most of the activities you engage in boring, or don't see much reason to get out of bed each morning. You may be thinking you're doing everything you're "supposed to." (Don't know what you don't know.) Why, then, would you feel disgruntled?

Another indication "This ain't it" is soft addictions. For example, do you zone out in front of the television or playing video games? Or are you a compulsive overeater?

Perhaps your addictions are more pronounced, such as excessive gambling, prescription and illegal drug or alcohol abuse, or other numbing activities. There are many "soft" and "hard" addictions that are signs you're unhappy with yourself or your current life circumstances.

Life Force Meter

Being in a situation where you are unhappy is normal for many people. You keep putting one foot in front of the other in your relationships, your job, and your family, thinking that's just the way it's supposed to be. I recently had someone ask me about the various job and career changes I made over my lifetime. I realized that none of those jobs excited me for any length of time. Yes, they were interesting, they offered advancement opportunities and greater pay, they offered me the opportunity to live in different parts of the country, and I worked with some amazing people. But on the "Life Force Meter," my needle was on the "drudge" side and far from the joy I yearned for. It wasn't the people, the jobs, or where I lived that decided where I felt on the "Life Force Meter." It was whether or not they were right for me.

After reading the W. H. Murray quote I mentioned in the Introduction, I thought about what I wanted to commit to. What would be exciting for me? I started to get a little depressed. "I just resigned from my job. Am I nuts?" my mind screamed. Initially, I thought I needed to have some grand purpose or passion to commit to – something along the lines of saving the world, or at least making a significant contribution. And I was coming up blank. It was frustrating.

Then I asked myself, "What do I enjoy doing?" I started a list, which included travel, dancing, baseball, racquetball, volleyball, playing board games and cards, being in nature, being with friends and family, being on/in/under the water, writing, being creative, making a difference. It wasn't long before I noticed a lot of travel-related activities appearing on my list. While I was going through this discernment process, I attended a presentation by a woman who had lived in the Alaska wilderness for a year. Alaska. It resonated with me. It wasn't saving the world, but I got excited about the prospect of traveling to Alaska and the Arctic Circle.

Just the thought of a trip to Alaska pushed my Life Force Meter to "I love life!" And that's when I committed. I didn't know how. I didn't know why. I did know that I felt excited and was coming alive with passion and purpose.

Setting the Course

Have you ever hopped in your car and just started driving with no particular destination in mind? I remember doing that a lot, especially when I was learning how to drive or when I moved to a new place. Sometimes it's pleasant just to wander and explore. It can be fun, and it can lead you to new people and places you would not otherwise have found. Traveling with no particular destination can also lead to unpredictable, unpleasant outcomes. It's something like life. If you don't care about the destination, any decision will do. However, you might not like the result.

In my life, I had achieved a lot in terms of higher education and progressively more responsible jobs, often receiving recognition along the way. On the surface, I probably seemed successful, and I mostly had fun. I met some awesome people. Yet I don't know that I could say my life had purpose or passion. So it was no surprise that I found myself in tears on that fateful afternoon before I quit my job and embarked on my Alaska adventure.

Without realizing it, I had recognized that something was missing in my life. I didn't know what it was. However, it felt freeing to enter that second stage of awareness, conscious incompetence, where I discovered there were things I didn't know. This new understanding opened the path of discovery.

Thanks to W. H. Murray's quote I uncovered an immutable, universal law at work in my life. You must be clear about what you want. When you are clear, Providence (God, Higher Power, Greater Intelligence, the Universe) will know what resources you need to reach your destination. Notice I said to be clear about what you want. If you focus on what you *don't* want, that will be what shows up. You *must* identify what you *do* desire.

I focused on what I wanted – Alaska. There were a lot of details – the "how" – to be dealt with. However, I discovered that my clarity of vision was the essential ingredient for me to achieve my goal of standing at the Arctic Circle. And I let everyone who would listen know about my dream. Because I was clear, because I was passionate, and because I was committed, I experienced "all manner of unforeseen incidents and meetings and material assistance" coming my way.

What Holds You Back

It's exciting to discover what you truly want in life. Many times, when that initial awareness comes, you want to run out and start making things happen. And at first, many things do start happening that support creating the life you envision. Wow! Your Life Force Meter is off the charts. But then, old, limiting beliefs, habits, addictions, or friends and relatives start to tug at your resolve, dragging you back into the "same ol' same ol'."

You might discover that those who you expected to be supportive are the ones who most want to hold you back. People in Twelve-Step programs experience these challenges as they free their lives from addictive behaviors. They've changed, and even though it is generally for the better, it can be threatening to the people around them. In your case, friends, family members or co-workers who start out supportive and delighted with the transformation sometimes begin questioning the wisdom of your decision, drop subtle innuendos, or become outright hostile. They had become comfortable with the old you. If you began transforming your life, they might feel threatened because they begin to see what's missing in their lives.

Sometimes your purpose and passion are strong enough to carry you through these challenges. Other times, your new direction is not yet compelling enough and sufficiently anchored in your subconscious to protect you and keep you on course to your new vision. So you fall back into the limiting beliefs that, like crabs in a barrel, claw to drag you back.

A story most Westerners are familiar with is the Biblical story of Jesus' birth. Mary wrapped the baby Jesus in swaddling clothes (or bands of cloth). Even today we wrap infants snugly in a blanket. It makes them feel safe and protected, as they were in their mothers' wombs. That's what your new idea, your new vision, your new passion is like. It requires protection and nurturing until it is strong enough to be revealed to the world.

Remember, some people don't like it when you become confident in yourself and become strong. Your confidence and strength remind them of their own insecurities and weaknesses. Don't let their envy slow you down or hold you back. Love them and keep moving forward. It's possible your example of living the life you love could be the beacon of hope and promise they need to transform their own lives.

Chapter III

INSPIRATION

"Be not afraid of greatness. some are born great,
some achieve greatness, and some have
greatness thrust upon 'em."
– William Shakespeare

Have you seen yourself yet? Regardless of your age, it's still possible to get caught up in other people's expectations or your self-imposed ones. You might avoid looking at what *you* want because of some deep-seated fear or insecurity. Or you might be caught by beliefs about your sex, skin color, ethnicity, socio-economic background, or religion. Then, of course, there are perceived obstacles such as the economy, who got elected president, where you live, or just general perceived turmoil around you. There are many circumstances and outside considerations that can hold you back from even thinking about what you would love.

If you're reading this book, you're already on your journey of self-discovery. You're already feeling the pull of your heart's desire – even if you haven't yet identified what that desire is. Congratulations! You are right where you're supposed to be. Your job is to be happy. The great thing about "happy" is that it's an inside job. No one and nothing (no thing) can make you happy or unhappy. Only you can. No matter what the songs say, no matter what the movies say, no matter what the negative news stories say, you're the one in charge.

I believe that each of us was given life to serve a very special and unique purpose. There's a contribution that only you can make in this world. Your brother can't make it, your sister can't make it, your best friend can't make it, and I can't make it. Only you can. It's *your* special contribution. If you're a person of faith, consider it God yearning to express through you as you. For others, it's simply a deep-seated, internal calling that can't be denied because it is you, the true you, aching to be revealed in the world.

Pharrell Williams' song *Happy* invites you to be happy. It doesn't stipulate that certain conditions be present, that you be in love, that you have a great job, that you just passed an important exam, or that you look attractive. It just says,

"I'm happy." No reason. "Can't nothing, bring me down, I said, Because I'm happy...."

"Happy" is what I invite you to be, starting now, with no outer reason. Be happy because that's what you are meant to be, because happy is a choice.

Thoughts & Ideas

Everyone has thoughts, and every thought contains an idea. It's the beauty of how we are wired as human beings. We can't be other than creative, idea-generating machines. It's in our DNA. That's the great news. The "you" you are meant to be is already within you, aching to be revealed. Yet you have resistance that has built up over your lifetime that discourages and suppresses those inspired, imaginative, energizing ideas from rising to the surface of your conscious mind and bursting forth into physical reality.

You are thinking every moment. Depending on where you currently are on the Life Force Meter, your thoughts might be negative, neutral, or positive. The amount of energy you invest depends on the emotion you are experiencing. For example, if you tend toward the lower end of the Life Force Meter, your energy will be low if you're feeling depressed or without hope. If you're feeling angry, your energy signature will be much higher, and it will be destructive. If you're feeling joy, you're on the positive side of the Life Force Meter, your energy signature will be of a higher vibration, and it will be creative and constructive.

We're focusing on ideas that come from the creative, constructive side of the spectrum. This is where you will find clues to your purpose and passion. This is where you will begin to see possibility and promise. This is where your true self begins to shine.

Everything is created twice – first in the mind, then in physical reality. The chair you're sitting on, the refrigerator where you keep your food, the car you drive – they all were first created in mind. They were an idea, an inspiration. If they hadn't been, they wouldn't exist.

The same principle applies to your health and well-being, your spiritual growth, and your emotions. First, you hold the idea. So if you hold the idea (belief) that your body is sickly, then that's what you'll experience. If you hold the idea that you're healthy, your body will respond accordingly. If you believe in omens and the "evil eye," you'll experience distress and even death if you encounter them. That's how powerful your mind is.

I mentioned earlier that happiness is an inside job. It's a decision you make. Yes, a decision. You will hear people say that they can't control their emotions. You might be one of them. This isn't true. Yes, there may be chemical imbalances in your body, but even these can be changed through the power of the thoughts and ideas you dwell on and harbor in your mind. There's an expression, "Thoughts held in mind produce after their kind." That means you'll experience results where you focus your thoughts, emotions, and energy.

You have the power. Perhaps you've been taught that outside circumstances dictate how your life will turn out. You may believe you're a victim of fate. None of this is true. You are the captain of your own ship. You are at the helm. You chart your life's course. You decide what to do when you encounter a storm. If your boat has sails, you decide what to do when the air is dead calm. You decide. You. You may decide to do nothing. You may change course. You may batten down the hatches and hide. You may fire up the auxiliary engines and continue on your original course. You may take advantage of a calm to do repairs, rest, or rejuvenate. It's your choice, your decision.

There are 1,440 minutes in a day, 525,600 minutes in a year. What you do with those precious minutes is up to you. Even in jail, people like the Apostle Paul, Nelson Mandela, and Martin Luther King, Jr. used their time to reflect, rejuvenate, write, and inspire. Thoughts and ideas flow continuously. They can be positive and uplifting or negative and depressing. They're creative or neutral. They're always present. Which ones will you choose?

Which ones will you dwell on? You create your life through your ideas and where you focus your thoughts. You have the power.

What Would You Love?

Has anyone ever asked you, "What would you love?" I've only been asked that question in the past few years. Wow! What would I love? Would I even dare think about living the life I would love? I knew I was living the life I was called to. But I never thought in terms of "Is this a life I love?" Professionally, I could answer "yes." But I realized there's more I wanted to do. Health-wise, I was generally satisfied, but "love"? No, there was more that I wanted in terms of physical vitality, strength, and weight. How about relationships? I have close, loving friendships that I value and hold dear. Yet here too, there was more that I wanted. Financially, I felt comfortable, yet there was certainly room for increased prosperity in my life. "Would it be all right if I had everything I could possibly want?" was a question I had to ask myself on the way to answering "What would I love?"

Why is it important to identify what you would love? After all, aren't you supposed to simply "buck up" and take what life hands you? Culturally, that's what many of us are taught. But does following that dictum create a life worth living? What would it be like to change the rules for everyone? What would it be like to start with you?

What would you love? Take a moment right now to ask yourself the question, "What would I love?"

Pause here and meditate on that question. "What would I love?"

Give yourself at least five minutes to be quiet with this question. Then *quickly* write down everything that comes to mind. No editing for whether it's practical, logical, or enlightened. Just write. I recommend you create a notebook or journal for this journey of discovery. This would be a good time to pull out your notebook and start using it, if you haven't already.

STOP! If you just kept reading, stop. You probably think you'll come back to this exercise later or don't see the value in it. If you have read this far, it's because you are hungry to make a change. You want to reengineer, reinvent, or reimagine your life. That means committing to doing the work. And the work starts here.

There's a reason I asked you to pause right now to consider "What would I love?" You are worth having the life you would love. Continuing to read without allowing yourself to consider what you would love is discounting the splendid person that you are. Take this opportunity to explore the inner voice that whispers lovingly of the wonders of the life you are meant to live. Pause, and ask, "What would I love?"

Maybe I Can

Yay! Congratulations if you took the time to reflect on "What would I love?" Just considering such a question is a significant and important step to creating that life. Writing it down is acknowledging and celebrating the inner yearning within. Writing what you would love is communicating to yourself and the universe that you're open and willing to claim and become who and what you are meant to be.

Take another moment now and acknowledge yourself for claiming this precious part of you – the part that dares to dream.

STOP! Did you do what I just asked? This exploration is about celebrating you. Pausing to savor your own aspirations and greatness is part of the journey.

Now that my mini-lecture is over, I invite you to look at what thoughts and emotions came up as you wrote down what you would love. Did you give yourself an internal "high five"? Did you watch in amazement and wonder as you wrote, not realizing you had such high hopes and desires in you? Or did you scoff at yourself, even abandoning the exercise as impractical and stupid, thinking "Who am I to think I could have this kind of a life?" Either way, congratulations! You're still reading, which means you're heading in the direction to claim your dreams and demonstrate your innate greatness.

Anchoring

Why did I ask you to write down your answers? Isn't it enough to simply think about it? The challenge is that your mind is constantly jumping from one thought to another, like a monkey jumping between tree limbs. That's why the Buddhists call it Monkey Mind. I call it mental mischief, like an overactive child (or puppy) being constantly distracted by the next shiny object. Writing down your dream helps prevent your doubts and fears from progressing from mental mischief to mental mayhem.

You write down what you would love as a first step in crossing the threshold between what you desire and what you actually experience. Writing your dreams gives you a foundation upon which to build. This is the beginning. There is more, much more, waiting to be birthed. This is the first crack in the delicate shell between possibility and reality.

Let me pause and share with you my definition of "reality." I remember attending various self-development seminars – the kind that help you get a glimpse of the remarkable soul you truly are. Inevitably, someone in the group would comment as the seminar was coming to a close, "Oh no. Now I have to return to the real world." Initially, I had the same thought, but then I realized the experience of my true self *was* the "real world." What I was returning to was an illusion created by the filters through which we view the world because of the programming we received from family, friends, teachers, bosses, church, and society over our lifetimes. The dream you're birthing is a glimpse into *your* real world.

Review what you wrote down as you answered the question, "What would I love?" What are you feeling? Are you excited? Doubtful? Are you filled with anticipation and possibility? Or are you wondering, "Who am I to have such dreams and aspirations?" These are normal reactions. The decision right now is to choose where you want to focus. Remember, your thought field is filled with infinite possibilities that include thoughts and beliefs that lift you up and those that drag you down. You have the power. Where do you want to concentrate your attention?

Having the idea isn't enough. Believing you could actually achieve your dream is key. Go beyond hope and embrace the possibility as your own. The children's story, *The Little Engine That Could*, illustrates the power of starting with "I think I can. I think I can." to the certainty of "I know I can." That you are reading this book is an example of my own journey of "I think I can write a book" to "I know I can" to "I did it!" I know that *you* can achieve your dream too.

This Could Be Fun!

Here's another concept that might be foreign to many of you. Not only might you be able to live the life you love, you might even have fun doing it! Try that thought on for a moment. "Gee, this might be fun!" There's enough in life that feels like obligation and responsibility. What would it be like if your life's purpose was fun? You might find it difficult to wrap your brain around this concept. Depending on your conditioning over a lifetime, you might not be able to accept that life could be easier, more enjoyable, and even exciting.

I propose that you can have fun. Just as being happy is a decision, so is having fun. I've had jobs in my life that included routine, repetitive, mundane activities. When I worked as a union organizer in Boston, we sent out weekly mailings to the people we wanted to join our bargaining unit. Imagine stuffing hundreds of envelopes every Friday evening. Drudgery, right? Well, I figured out a way to make it fun. Even though there were several of us working, I set up a competition with myself. How efficiently and quickly could I fold the letters, then stuff and seal them in the envelopes? Just setting up this simple inner contest was all it took to turn drudgery into a sense of accomplishment and fun. Plus, we finished faster, so we could be on our way to have other fun.

Start thinking about how your dream would be fun. To strengthen that sense of fun, look at something in your life that has the appearance of "not fun" and get creative with ways you could make it an enjoyable activity or interaction.

Why look at both your dream life and your current life as fun? It's all about energy. As you raise your vibration to a higher, more joyful level in one area of your life, that same energy permeates all areas of your life. If you hate what you're doing now, look for one area in which to create fun. Are you making collection calls all day? Do you make "cold calls" to enroll people in a particular product or service? Do you run the same machinery hour after hour, day after day? Do you work around death and dying? Have you been long-term unemployed and have given up? Are you the executive everyone relies on to solve a crisis? No matter what situation you find yourself in, look for something fun or rewarding.

As you discover and focus on fun, you'll experience a shift, both in the activity and in other areas of your life. You become a magnet for more fun. Your attitude becomes more positive. Your health improves. More opportunities open up to you. You begin to live a possibility-based life, recognizing that your "real world" is living the life you love.

Chapter IV

CLARITY

"I can teach anybody how to get what they want out of life. The problem is that I can't find anybody who can tell me what they want."
– Mark Twain

In the previous chapter, we began asking the question, "What would I love?" I encourage you to read your dream every day – in the morning when you awaken and at night before you retire. Add to it as you continue uncovering your inner yearnings. This is a living, breathing document, not something static that holds you down and limits your creativity and life. As you tap your inner greatness, more will emerge to be cultivated, celebrated, and expanded. Reading what you wrote and expanding it will take your dream into your very cells so that you become one with who and what you truly are.

What Brings You Joy?

When do you come alive? Is it when you're dancing? Being with your children (or children in general)?

Watching the sun rise? Travel? Gardening? What do you find truly amazing?

This might seem repetitious of the "What would you love?" question I've already asked. But this time, I'm asking what it is about your life *right now* that you enjoy. You don't want to "throw the baby out with the bathwater," so this section invites you to identify what you love and want to cherish and grow in your life right now. Looking at what you already enjoy, but may not have identified, will also help you solidify the future you're creating and claiming.

You may love helping people, creating beautiful music, or feeling safe in your home. What do you want to keep in your life? Ask yourself, "What brings me joy?" Take the time now to meditate on this question and write down your answers. Use the same notebook or journal you started when you answered the question, "What would I love?"

Again, STOP! if you continued reading without pausing to ask yourself, "What brings me joy?" If you're skimming over these questions, what is coming up for you that prevents you from looking within? Is it the mental mischief we talked about in Chapter III? Remember, mental mischief only shows up and threatens to become mental mayhem when you're up to something big. When you remain in the same old patterns, beliefs, and activities that held you in a rut of sameness, inactivity, and lethargy, mental mischief has no reason to trouble you.

What's Your Inner Truth?

What are the values or Inner Truths that you base your life on? Do you treasure love, honesty, integrity, and creativity? Are you in touch with what's important to you?

You might think you're in touch with your Inner Truth until someone asks, "What's important to you?" Or until you find yourself in distress, wondering why life is feeling uncomfortable, stressful, or in crisis. When the latter happens, it's usually because you're not being coherent with who you truly are. This occurs when you're not clear about your Inner Truth or when you've allowed conditions to run your life.

Let's take a moment now to get in touch with your Inner Truth. First, take out your notebook and create two columns. In the first column, list the people you admire most. The list could include people currently in your life, historical figures, athletes, politicians, spiritual leaders, even cartoon or mythical figures. Who do you admire? List five to ten people.

When you have completed your list, consider what it is you admire about each person. For example, if Dr. Martin

Luther King, Jr. is on your list, perhaps you admire his leadership, vision, loyalty, and dedication. If your mother is on your list, perhaps you value her love, fairness, creativity, vision, and dedication.

After you finish writing down the attributes you admire about each of the individuals on your list, read them and begin circling the values that recur most often. Perhaps leadership, integrity, love, passion, and honesty stand out. Or perhaps power, imagination, love, versatility, and consistency stand out for you. There are no right or wrong answers, only what resonates with you.

Illustration

Person I Admire	Attributes
Martin Luther King, Jr.	Visionary, Leader, Charismatic, Dedicated, Passionate, Courageous
Joan Smith	Leader, Intelligent, Powerful, Loving, Visionary, Charismatic, Courageous
Mom	Loving, Caring, Dedicated, Persevering, Spiritual, Passionate
Mother Theresa	Courageous, Spiritual, Loving, Leader, Caring, Passionate
Nelson Mandela	Leader, Intelligent, Powerful, Dedicated, Visionary, Charismatic, Courageous,

After you have identified the values you admire in your list of people, circle those attributes that seem to repeat or that especially resonate with you. For this exercise, limit the number to five or seven.

Person I Admire	*Attributes*
Martin Luther King, Jr.	Visionary, Leader, Charismatic, Dedicated, Passionate, Courageous
Joan Smith	Leader, Intelligent, Powerful, Loving, Visionary, Charismatic, Courageous
Mom	Loving, Caring, Dedicated, Persevering, Spiritual, Passionate
Mother Theresa	Courageous, Spiritual, Loving, Leader, Caring, Passionate
Nelson Mandela	Leader, Intelligent, Powerful, Dedicated, Visionary, Charismatic, Courageous, Passionate, Loving

Now take a 3x5 card and write at the top, "This is my Inner Truth. I am." List the attributes you identified. Then at the bottom of your card write, "I know these are mine, because I see them in others."

In the above illustration, the attributes that stand out are Visionary, Loving, Passionate, Courageous, Leader, and Intelligent.

The card would read:

This is my Inner Truth. I am
    Visionary
    Loving
    Passionate
    Courageous
    Leader
    Intelligent

Any surprises? What's on your list? Perhaps your list has people such as Magic Johnson, Michael Phelps, Eminem, Tom Brady, John Stewart, and your father. So your list might include athletic, prosperous, creative, fun, insightful, and accepting. You would write,

This is my Inner Truth. I am
    Athletic
    Fun
    Prosperous
    Creative
    Insightful
    Accepting

The first time I completed this exercise was when Maria Nemeth, Ph.D., founder of the Academy for

Coaching Excellence, presented it to my ministerial class in 2000. I cried when I was asked to say, "I know these are mine, because I see them in others." My initial list included loving, charismatic, spiritual, intelligent, leader, integrity, and kind. "How could these wonderful attributes be in me?" I wondered. A lifetime of being told all that was wrong with me had made its mark. This one exercise touched my soul like no other.

You're often told that when you dislike certain traits in other people, it's because they're the negative aspects of yourself that you abhor. What you seldom hear is that when you *admire* something in other people, it's because you have those attributes in yourself. You wouldn't recognize those positive aspects in others if you didn't have the essence of them already within you. They wouldn't have had a place to land ("landing page") in your consciousness.

Your list is not static. You'll find that your lists of both people and attributes can change over the years. As you evolve, you become open to new and wonderful possibilities. Your landing page expands to include more uplifting, higher-vibration truths. You'll discover that things you used to find annoying in other people no longer exist for you because you're no longer on that lower vibration. As you rise in consciousness and vibration and increasingly see the good in others (even those you saw negatively before), you raise everyone up – yourself and those around you.

Your Epitaph

If you were to write your own epitaph, what would you want it to say? What would you like to be remembered for? Does this sound maudlin? It's not. Rather, this is an opportunity to zero in on the contribution you want to make in the world. Were you that quiet presence that people sought when they were troubled or wanted to share their successes? Did you climb Mt. Everest? Did you hike the Appalachian Trail or spend your days sitting on the beach, enjoying the sunsets? Did you raise a family? Were you a loving son or daughter? Were you a teacher, leader, or volunteer? Did you invent something that made life better for others? Did you give your time, money, and talent to causes you believed in? What would you like to be remembered for? Include this in your notebook as you write your epitaph.

Review what you just wrote. Did you uncover areas where you're not yet living the life you would love? Did further areas of longing or discontent surface because there's a gap between where you are and where your heart guides you? Or are you right on track? Either way, acknowledge and celebrate every insight you have. Give yourself a hug. Put a big gold star, or perhaps a heart, in your notebook. These insights and discoveries you're making are laying the foundation for living the life you would love.

Let Your Light Shine!

Congratulations! You're opening the door to the magnificent, amazing you that I know you are. Some of you haven't participated in the exercises presented so far. Others have rushed through them. And a few of you have leaped in with both feet! All of you are still reading. That means you want to get in touch with the life you would love, the life yearning to be experienced through you. Savor this moment. Acknowledge to yourself that you're showing the world your willingness to be a shining star.

We have had many great teachers in the world over the centuries. One of them, Jesus of Nazareth, proclaimed, "You are the light of the world. A city set on a hill cannot be hidden; nor does anyone light a lamp and put it under a basket, but on the lampstand, and it gives light to all who are in the house. 'Let your light shine...'" (Matthew 5:14-16) No matter your faith tradition, this declaration applies to you.

You are the light! The world is a lesser place when you hide it. By allowing yourself to shine – and be the best, most magnificent being you are meant to be – you bless the world, and you contribute mightily to its transformation. You make the world a better place with each thought, each word, and each action. Your greatness lies within you. Are you willing to express it and create a better world? Are you ready to radiate your light?

Stake Your Claim

Up to this point, I've invited you to open your mind to how magnificent you are. You dared to dream: "What would I love?" You honored what you already enjoy about your life when you asked, "What brings me joy?" You looked within and uncovered the Inner Truths you hold dear and make you special to humanity. And you wrote your own epitaph, identifying the contributions you want to make in this lifetime. Now it's time to stake your claim to the life you would love.

Years ago, when I was studying for my coaching certification, my instructor told me to write a letter to a trusted friend dated eighteen months in the future. I was to describe where I lived, my work, my relationships, my health and well-being, my abundance, my play, and whatever else I wanted to see happen in my life. I was to write this as if it had already happened.

At the time I was on sabbatical between ministries. I had released most of my possessions, put the rest in storage, and hit the road in my Subaru Outback. I had my camping gear, my computer, my cell phone, a few clothes and books, and no idea where or when I would land. I said, "No, I can't do this. I have no idea what I'll be doing in eighteen months." My instructor gave me a choice (we always have choices): do the assignment and finish my training or not do it and leave the program. I did the assignment, begrudgingly and with little passion.

Basically, I made it up, e-mailed it, and never looked at it again – until a couple of years later when I found it in my computer. I was amazed at how much of what I had "made up" simply to get my instructor off my back had come true – how much had come from an inner voice that I hadn't yet listened to. I share this story because now it's your turn to step into the future and look back at all that you've accomplished.

Remember the W. H. Murray quotation from the Introduction? "Until one is committed..." Here is your opportunity to commit to your greatness, to proclaim to the world how amazing you are, and to place your light for all to see.

Imagine yourself eighteen months in the future. You are reflecting back on the last year and a half. You're filled with joy and gratitude for all you have accomplished. You decide to share your experiences, and you celebrate with a dear friend in a letter. You begin with, "I'm so happy and grateful for these past eighteen months." Then start sharing what you accomplished in your career/vocation, in your relationships, in your health and physical vitality, in your fun times, in your finances, and in where you live. Remember, it has already happened, so use the past tense. Include your feelings and five senses.

For example,

"I'm so happy and grateful to tell you the exciting things that have happened in my life over the last year and a half. I am grateful for all the blessings I've experienced. First, I landed my dream job as _____ for XYZ Company. Everyone there is friendly and supportive. I have the opportunity to be creative and innovative, and I've already received a promotion and raise. My work area is spacious and inviting, with large windows that let in sunlight throughout the day.

I love my home. I repainted the living room with soft hues of green and added floral pillows to brighten up the sofa and chairs. I planted rose bushes along the walkway to my front door and make a point to literally stop and smell the roses every day. I started taking dance lessons last spring and met an amazing dance partner who has become an important part of my life. We share the same values and enjoy the same leisure activities. We even started our own mini-study group because we discovered we're interested in the same type of literature. We visited Ireland in the fall. Oh, how beautiful it was. The people were friendly, the music joyful and uplifting, and the food satisfying and fresh...."

Get the idea? What would you love? What do you enjoy in your life already? What are your Inner Truths? What contribution do you want to make to the world? Now stake your claim by giving your dream the fullness of your imagination, passion, and commitment. Be specific, using clear, unambiguous terms that the universe (God, Creator, your angels, your guardians or however you call your higher power) will understand and have no choice but to respond to by bringing you all the ideas, people, and resources needed to make your vision come alive in your everyday life. At the end of your statement, say, "This or something better." Date it eighteen months in the future, and sign your name to it. Remember, Name it! Claim it! And Proclaim it!

As you continue working the exercises in this book, go to www.EmbracingGreatness.com for free downloads, gifts, and updates.

Chapter V

DEEP DIVE

"As human beings, greatness is not
so much in being able to remake the world
as in being able to remake ourselves."
– Gandhi

In 1984 I moved from Boston, Massachusetts, which is on the ocean, to Tucson, Arizona, which is in a desert. So of course, I learned how to S.C.U.B.A. dive after I moved to the desert. It seemed illogical to my friends in the Northeast, but to my new friends in the desert, it made perfect sense. First I learned from instructor lectures and textbooks. Then the instructor took us to a large pool where we got the feel of the diving mask and snorkel, wearing a B.C.D. (buoyancy control device), swimming with the large flippers that divers wear, and other diving-related exercises.

There was a written exam. I passed. And then came the practicum, but not in the pool where we had practiced. It was time to meet the ocean. Or to be specific, the Sea of Cortez, which was ocean enough for me since (a) it was salty (I grew up with freshwater lakes), (b) I couldn't see the other shore, and (c) it was deeper than anything I had ever experienced before.

I remember our first exercise away from the shore, with no bottom to be seen, and nasty, gritty salt water getting into my eyes, nose, mouth, and ears. Panic. Fears I didn't know I had started to surface. Ocean swells are different from the lapping lake ripples I was accustomed to. And we didn't have sea monsters in the lake. Snapping turtles maybe, baby sunfish nipping at your heels perhaps, but certainly no sharks, stingrays, or moray eels. The salt and wave action bothered me most. I started hyperventilating. I made my discomfort known to the instructor. She swam over to me, put more air in my BCD so I didn't have to worry about staying afloat, had me lie back, and told my diving buddy to make sure I didn't drift out to sea while she finished our drill.

I'm a good swimmer. In fact, I often tease friends that I'm part fish because I so enjoy being on the water, in the water, and under the water – freshwater, that is, which would make me a freshwater fish. However, the S.C.U.B.A. drills we went through were the opening to a deeper experience with the water – in this case, the ocean.

I could have insisted that I be taken back to shore when I felt my initial panic. But it was more interesting to me to expand my relationship with the water (the ocean and all the mysteries waiting to unfold) than it was to give into the experience of "panic." I was more interested in overcoming any underlying fears that would have caused me to give up the possibilities of ocean diving than to stay in my freshwater comfort zone.

In the previous chapter on Clarity, you began the process of identifying your dream. It's starting to take form. The experience may have felt exhilarating – or deep-seated doubts and fears may have surfaced. The process of writing down your dream is an initial step, a way to begin anchoring your dream so that mental mischief will have less power to sway you from achieving your dream.

You may even be getting through the first few steps easily. And then, panic. You're no longer in your safe, comfortable wading pool. You're stepping out, or should I say "swimming" into uncharted territory. This is where all the messages you've received over the years from others and from yourself start surfacing. If you were consistently and continuously told you weren't smart enough, tall enough, pretty enough, tough enough, talented enough, rich enough, etc., and you believed it, your subconscious accepted these "not enough" statements as truth.

Identifying Your Negative Self-Talk

I remember once overhearing a man in a shopping mall tell his adolescent son, "Don't be so stupid. Can't you do anything right?" As the child squirmed and demurred, the father continued with a barrage of "You're stupid," "You'll never amount to anything," and similar comments. My heart went out to the boy. He was already being programmed to believe that he was stupid and worthless. He was already being subjected to public humiliation and shame.

Ouch.

Has anything like that ever happened to you?

A parent, teacher, or other "authority figure" puts you down. Your classmates or the neighborhood kids razz you and you end up feeling awkward and inadequate when you're around them. Or you do very well on a test or sporting event, but someone else gets the attention because he or she did just a little bit better.

The scarring that these experiences cause can go deep. You might laugh it off and strut onward with bravado and a confident swagger. Yet inside you feel insecure, incompetent, or inadequate. Many of us have been there. And no matter how much you shine in the different areas of your life, what you notice is where you don't measure up to some arbitrarily imposed standard, very often inflicted by someone who feels insecure or scared.

Then there are the comments that might have been made to you about your physical looks. Your teeth are crooked, you're too fat (thin), your hair's too curly (straight, thin, coarse), you slouch, and on and on and on. Nowadays that's often called bullying, yet it's not just comments from your peers, it's also judgment heaped upon you by authority figures throughout your life. Some think they're being helpful. Others are unaware of the damaging impact their comments will have on you.

When I graduated from Albany State University with my bachelor's degree, I lived for a time in a boarding house while I substitute taught in the Albany public schools. Across the street was a family of five. If I were to show you their pictures, you might label them as plain looking, even unattractive. The mother and father were bright, positive people, and I enjoyed visiting them. Their son and two daughters all wore thick eyeglasses – the kind that would probably cause some to call them "four eyes." And they were a little overweight and had acne. In short, they wouldn't have been called "pretty."

Yet these children were being raised to see themselves as smart and beautiful. I remember seeing the father taking each child's hands, looking them right in the eye, and asking questions such as, "Who's the prettiest little girl in the world?" to which his daughter would respond loudly with great joy on her face, "I am!" Then the father would ask, "And who's the smartest little girl in the world?" and again she gleefully shouted, "I am!" He did the same drill with each daughter and with his son. How beautiful to see such love and light bestowed on those children, and to see them grow in confidence and understanding of how amazing they were.

Not your childhood? Nope, not mine either. But it brings home the point that our programming on how good or not-so-good we are started early and was reinforced over the years – first, by those around us, then, by our own negative thinking and belief systems.

It's Your Time!

You've probably heard the saying, "Better the devil you know than the devil you don't." Have you ever held back because this belief resonated with you? Now that you've gotten in touch with your dream, it's time to leave the "devil" behind and move forward into your dream.

One way to leave the devil behind is to recognize that when you start feeling apprehensive, it's because you're stepping outside your comfort zone to claim the life you would love. Remember when you studied European history in school? Before Columbus discovered the Americas, most Europeans believed the world was flat. If you sailed too far, you'd fall off. So the sailors of the day clung to the shores of the land they knew. Maps were drawn with sea monsters at the edge of the known world. The world ended with the words "Terra Incognita" (unknown territory).

But there were a few visionaries who believed there was something worth discovering beyond what was already known. Christopher Columbus was one of them. He approached many ship owners and country rulers, asking them to believe in his vision and provide him with ships and manpower to explore the unknown. They all said "no." Finally, King Ferdinand and Queen Isabella of Spain agreed to sponsor him. But their confidence only extended to giving Columbus old ships, and crew members taken mostly from the prisons.

How scary it must have been for the crew and officers as they left the known world behind. But they faced their fears and sailed into terra incognita. They changed the world. How about you? What's your terra incognita? Are you ready to release the devil you know and embrace something new and exciting? Are you ready to recognize that there's something greater for you than the life you already know?

There are two main indicators that it's time to follow your yearnings and step into the life you would love. First, you feel excited and exhilarated. Second, your doubts and fears show up. Mental mischief turns into mental mayhem. Although your inner longing guides you to something greater, the old programming tries to pull you back – like crabs in a barrel will try to pull back any brave crab that tries to escape.

Affirming Your Truth

Are you ready to release your negative self-talk? Are you ready to claim your greatness? Are you ready to live the life you would love?

Let's begin with the basics – the dream you identified in the chapter on Clarity. To take it deeper, look at your eighteen-month letter. Break down your dream in the following areas:

Where you live.

What's your geographic location – urban, rural, suburban? Do you live in a house or apartment? Do you own or rent? How many bedrooms, baths? Are there gardens surrounding your home? Or do you live on a boat, in a recreational vehicle?

Relationships.

Are you married? Single? Do you have close friends? Are your relationships supportive? Loving? Stimulating? Exciting? Mellow?

Career/Vocation/Volunteerism.

What is your work or career? What is your talent and how do you contribute it? Expertise?

Fun/Recreation.

Do you enjoy travel? Where? How often? What mode(s) of travel? How about dancing – what kind? Water sports?

Physical Vitality/Health.

How physically fit are you? How's your health? Can you run a four-minute mile or walk a mile in 20 minutes? Are you heart healthy? Have you overcome physical health challenges?

Spiritual.

What is your connection with your higher power/God? Your spiritual practices? Do you meditate? Pray? Participate in a particular spiritual community?

This is where you dig deeper into your dream. Again, as you describe every aspect of your vision, write as if it has already happened. This is how you anchor your dream in your cellular memory as if it has already happened. This step is important. Remember my assignment with my coach? Even though I didn't look at my eighteen-month letter, much of it came to pass. Imagine how much more I would have accomplished if I had worked with it as I'm inviting you to?

Activate the Law of Attraction

"Hold a picture of yourself long and
steady enough in your mind's eye, and
you will draw toward it."
– Napoleon Hill

In 2004, I was invited to a special showing of the movie *What the Bleep Do We Know!?* One of the movie's filmmakers was present to share how the movie came about and answer any questions. An audience member was vehemently opposed to the principles presented. After expressing her feelings, she stomped down the stairs toward the filmmaker. I held my breath, wondering if she would strike him. Instead, she left the theater.

This woman was upset with the concept that we have authority over our lives. To her, everything was "God's will," and what the movie presented was blasphemy. My reaction was different. I celebrated the creativity and clarity with which the filmmakers revealed the quantum field hidden behind what we consider to be our normal, waking reality. The main character, Amanda, discovered that the fundamental premises upon which she had based her life – and her opinions of others – were amiss. Instead of being a helpless victim to outside conditions and circumstances, she learned to release her limiting beliefs and fears and begin the process of being the creative force in her own life. She begins the journey from victim to victor, from emotional muddle to spiritual mastery.

That's what you're doing as you define and refine your inner longings and deep desires. By taking this deeper dive, you activate the law of attraction, alluded to in the quote from W. H. Murray.

Some of you will stop at this point, thinking all you need to do is have the thought of something greater for your life. "I don't have to write anything down. I've got it all in my head." The challenge here is that our thoughts are easily jumbled and swayed by our inner mental mischief and our outer conditions and naysayers. You deserve the life you desire. By diving deeper, then defining and refining your dream, you open the floodgates to attracting all the resources – mental, physical, and spiritual – that you need to make your dream come true.

The law of attraction activates your magnetizing power on all levels. We all use the law, whether we're aware of it or not. Just look at your life. It reflects and attracts what you focus on. If you focus on what you don't like or your language is filled with "I can't," "I'm not good enough," or "Yes, but," you'll attract lack, frustration, and "not enough." If you focus on – and emotionalize – your desires, "providence" will move and bring to you all you need and all that you desire.

Gratitude & the Law of Attraction

Have you ever encountered someone who constantly complained? There's always something wrong. It's either too hot or too cold. Their spouse never remembers their birthday. Traffic's too congested. Or they blame other people or outer conditions for being late, making them fat because of their great cooking, or keeping them in poverty because "those damn bankers" are causing a recession.

You know these people. Perhaps you're one of them? Their focus is on what's not to their liking. The negative energy they generate repels their good. When they (or you) focus on what is perceived as wrong or missing, they (or you) will attract more of the same. Have you found yourself caught in this trap?

It's called the Law of Attraction. You attract what you concentrate on. Focus on what you *don't* like, and *that* will increase. Tired of things going "wrong"? It's easy to turn it around. It's called gratitude. If you think there's nothing to be grateful for, you would be wrong. No matter what the outer appearance may be, there's always a kernel of good embedded in the situation. Your job is to take a deep dive and find the good. And once you find the good – draw on the feeling of gratitude.

Is it too hot? Focus on how wonderful the sun is. Your spouse never remembers your birthday? Focus on how much he or she cares for you the other 364 days of the year. Traffic congested? What a great opportunity to listen to an uplifting CD. Lost your job? Be grateful for the opportunity to explore new possibilities.

Get the picture? Even if a condition appears upsetting on the surface, somewhere there's a kernel to be grateful for. And as you focus on that kernel, it expands to become a gold nugget.

Pull out your notebook. List five things you can easily be grateful for. Then list five things that might be painful or stressful. Look at each item of this second list and ask yourself, "What kernel in this situation can I be grateful for?" Be peaceful with the question. If nothing comes to you, ask your higher power for help. Even if it's as simple as "I made it through the day," write it down.

At first, it might be a challenge to find "good" in otherwise challenging conditions, but you'll discover that the more you exercise your gratitude muscle, the more you'll become a magnet for a continuous and growing stream of good in your life. Good can come in the form of more loving relationships, a more rewarding and higher-paying job, better health and physical vitality, unexpected invitations to fun activities with people you love, or inspiration for a creative project you've been working on.

There's no mystery to the power of gratitude and its mighty magnetic force. As you continue your practice of keeping a gratitude journal as part of your notebook, you'll more fully live the life you would love.

"Develop an attitude of gratitude, and give thanks for everything that happens to you, knowing that every step forward is a step toward achieving something bigger and better than your situation."

– Brian Tracy

Chapter VI

FORGIVENESS

"When you forgive someone, you dismantle
your structures of knowing about him or her.
You lay down your weapons and armor
and proceed onward. You lighten up."
– Maria Nemeth, Ph.D.

"Only the brave know how to forgive."
– Laurence Sterne

"It's one of the greatest gifts you
can give yourself, to forgive.
Forgive everybody."
– Maya Angelou

Why Forgiveness?

Have you ever heard the saying, "I'll forgive, but I'll
never forget"? That's the same as saying, "I won't forgive."
Or, "I'm not willing to forgive and let go." It's the holding
on that's the obstacle. When the disciples asked Jesus how
many times they should forgive, Jesus responded, "Seventy

times seven." Did he mean that literally? No. Jesus meant for you to do your forgiveness work and release feelings of hurt, anger, or any other negative emotion tied to a person or incident for as long it takes. Only then will you free up the negative energy that is holding you back.

Forgiveness might be necessary for another individual, for an occurrence (for example, the economy, a hurricane, a traffic jam that makes you miss a job interview, a service call), or yourself. Yes, yourself.

There are many books on forgiveness and many processes taught. If you've never read any of these books, you either don't see the need for forgiveness or you think you've done all the forgiveness work necessary and there's no need to revisit the question.

I remember a woman who was suffering from mercury poisoning. It was caused initially by dental work. It was worsened by her own attempts at self-healing. By the time she came to me, she didn't see any hope. She was further despondent because she wanted to re-experience a blissful moment when she had felt one with God. This reconnection eluded her, and she was frustrated and angry that she could not again have this feeling of bliss with God. She wanted answers.

After praying with her, I asked, "Can you forgive the dentist whose actions started the mercury poisoning in the first place?" "Of course I can't!" she replied vehemently. "Could you consider the possibility that you could forgive him?" "NO!" I worked with her all the way down to "Could you consider the possibility that someday, years in the future, you could consider that you might finally be able to forgive him?" "Absolutely not" was her response.

What do you think the possibility of her healing from the mercury poisoning or finding her bliss with God was? Until she could forgive that dentist, it's unlikely she would ever heal.

Do you have similar circumstances in your life? An area where you feel you can't forgive? If yes, you're blocking your good, whether in relationships, health, work, joy, love, or prosperity.

How do you forgive? The first step is deciding to forgive. Even if you see no reason to be the one to do the forgiving, decide anyway. Simply making the decision will start opening blocked energy that is keeping you from your good.

Forgiveness Begins Within You

It's not just others that need forgiveness. Sometimes you need to forgive yourself. There may be something you did or didn't do that had repercussions that hurt someone else or caused you to fail at something that's important to you. Remember in the chapter on Clarity when you identified your Inner Truths? When you're not aligned with those Truths, you're no longer being coherent with who you truly are. Feelings of self-loathing or disappointment can build – only to hold you back.

Thoughts that you need to forgive lie in the judgment you've made that you need to forgive a person or situation. What's behind your feeling that you need to forgive or not forgive? Usually, the judgment is that someone has done something "wrong." He or she might have stolen, cheated, lied, harmed, etc. What's the meaning you place on that action (or lack of action)? If you label it bad, reprehensible, or unforgivable, it's simply a sign that some basic need within you is not being met by the other person's actions or the outer circumstance.

Years ago there was a television police program called *Dragnet.* When the detective interviewed someone, he would always stop them if they started giving their interpretation of the event. He would say something like "The facts, ma'am, just the facts." When something happens that disturbs you, what are the facts? Single those out first. Then look at the interpretation you've placed on those facts.

Next, ask yourself, "What need of mine was not met when Joe said 'X' or when the power went out or when the recession hit?" Was your need for safety not met? Was your need for understanding not met? Was your need for sustenance not met? What basic, universal human need was not met? (See *Nonviolent Communication: A Language of Life* by Marshall Rosenburg, PhD or www.cnvc.org for more in-depth study of this concept.)

Once you get in touch with the need that wasn't met, look at the feelings or emotions that arose as a result. The feelings are about you. They reflect the filters and judgment that you placed on the original incident. The judgment and emotions sap your energy and put you into a place of unforgiveness and blockage.

That blockage becomes a major obstacle to attracting good into your life and in revealing your answer to the question, "What would I love?" That's what happened to the woman with mercury poisoning. By the time she visited me, her vibration was so low and her energy so depleted, the only thing that would have lifted her up was being willing to forgive.

Any negative emotion will prevent you from shining your light brightly. Imagine a pipe flowing out of a pond. Its purpose is to keep the flow of water moving so the pond doesn't get stagnant. Now imagine that twigs, dirt, and dead plant life start getting stuck in the pipe. What happens? The flow becomes a trickle until it finally stops.

Now imagine that you are at the receiving end of that pipe, and the pond is the source of your good. You depend on that pipe remaining open and free of impediments for your abundance to flow to you.

Anger, resentment, fear, and "unforgiveness" (lack of forgiveness) are like the twigs, dirt, and dead plants in the pipe. There is an abundance waiting to rush to you, yet you block it because you don't want to or don't see the need to forgive.

That Person No Longer Exists

Whether forgiving someone else or yourself, it's important to remember that you're no longer the same people. The person who did (or didn't do) the thing you are upset about is gone. We're always evolving.

This same principle applies to conflicts between families, ethnic and religious groups, and countries. The story of the Hatfields and the McCoys lives on. When I first heard about their feud, I remember thinking how silly it was to hold onto something that had happened generations ago. Yet that's part of the human consciousness. You and I might not be able to directly influence what happens between families, cultures, or countries. We can, however, do our own forgiveness work. In so doing, we shift the energy and vibration for ourselves and for those in our immediate sphere of influence. That raises their vibration, which affects those around them. It's the ripple effect. It begins with you and me.

Exercise Your Forgiveness Muscles

Tense up every muscle of your body. Go ahead. Every muscle from your forehead down to your toes. Squint your eyes. Clench your jaw and neck. Contract your chest. Tense your arms and hands. Pull in your abdomen as far as it will go. Squeeze your glutes, your thigh muscles, your knees and calves, and finally, your feet and toes. Go ahead – tense every muscle. Now hold it. Keep holding it. Hold it.

Now release. How does that feel? While you tensed your entire body, could you do anything else? Could you walk or talk? Could you embrace a loved one or experience joy? No, of course not. All your attention was on keeping your body tense. That's what unforgiveness is like – only on an emotional, mental, and spiritual level. You have focused all your attention on something that will hold you back.

When you released all that body tension, what did that feel like? Release? Relief? Like you were opening up? When you released your body's tension, were you then free to move forward with another physical activity? Think about something else? Yes, of course.

That's what forgiveness is like for your emotional, mental, and spiritual well-being.

Can you now see how not forgiving is a major obstacle to achieving any goal? If your goal is a loving relationship, how can you be loving when you're holding onto anger and resentment? If your goal is financial prosperity, how can you be prosperous when so much energy (think tensed body) is focused away from your goal? If your desire is to retire and live peacefully, how is that possible when you have disharmonious feelings within?

When a negative feeling arises, go within and discover what need has not been met. Honor that need. Acknowledge that you are experiencing these feelings.

Often just getting in touch with your unmet needs will reveal issues in other areas of your life that may require addressing. Your disquiet with another individual's action might be part of a pattern in your life that you have not yet recognized – a pattern that has kept you from experiencing abundance in your life. Isn't it time to look within, rather than trying to lay blame and responsibility on other people or on conditions?

Remember, when you're pointing a finger of blame, retribution, or anger at someone or something else, three fingers are pointing back at you. (Notice your thumb is keeping them in place so you have the opportunity to look at your own issues.)

Taking this internal look will help you make your decision to forgive. It will give you a new perspective for viewing the situation. It will give you some breathing room.

Do It Now

EXERCISE 1

After you decide to forgive, write down the situation that requires your forgiveness. It might be something simple such as someone cut you off in traffic or stepped in front of you in a long line at the airport. It might be more complex, involving physical or verbal abuse. Perhaps it's a downturn in the economy, being deployed overseas, the weather, or your car having serious mechanical problems.

Journal Time:

Write it down. The writing gives it substance, rather than having it be some ethereal fantasy memory floating around in your mind. It's remarkable how, when we let things jump around in our minds, they become more and more intense, aggravating, and larger than life. Write it down.

Next, write down every conceivable bad thing about the situation or what the person did. Write down how it hurt you, how it inconvenienced you, how it was just plain wrong, immoral, or disgusting. Get creative. And throw it all up.

Throw up every minute aspect of what happened. Did the downturn in the economy put you out of a job? Did you lose a relationship? Did you lose a limb and experience great emotional trauma? Write it all down.

When you think you're finished writing, keep writing. Empty yourself. Take a break and come back to your list. Did you forget anything? Keep writing.

Now that you see all that you've been holding onto, take a few moments and ask yourself some questions.

- Have I laid down everything that I've been holding onto?
- Am I willing to release all this energy that I held onto and that is holding me back?
- Am I willing to forgive?
- Am I willing to release this energy now and forever?

Your answer might be "no" to some of these questions, especially the last one. Be at peace with your answers, whether they are "yes" or "no."

If your answer is "no," perhaps there's more for you to release. Be willing to return to what you wrote down and add to it later. Simply by going through this exercise initially, you have already released a large amount of pent-up anger and resentment. You have already freed some of the energy trapped in the prison of unforgiveness. When your answer is "yes," burn or shred the paper and affirm "I release and I let go. I am free."

EXERCISE 2

This exercise can be practiced anywhere, at any time. If you were unable to release your feelings of anger and resentment in Exercise 1, this would be a good complementary practice for releasing the last of any residual negative energy you may still be holding.

When It's People:

Visualize the individual against whom you feel anger, resentment, dislike, or hatred. That person did something that hurt you or someone you care about. Notice how you feel – and the negative energy you're experiencing – when you think of them.

Now visualize someone you love and care deeply for. It might be a child, your spouse or sweetheart, a best friend, a teacher, or a beloved pet. Notice how you feel when you think of this beloved one, and how expansive and light your energy is.

The Interrupt/Substitute Practice: When you find yourself thinking about the person for whom you have negative energy, immediately bring to mind the image of who you love. If you are angry with Bill, as soon as you think of "Bill," substitute the image of "Mary," whom you love. Notice a shift in energy when you interrupt the negative energy that arises around the image of "Bill" and substitute the image and energy you feel toward "Mary." At first, you might find yourself quickly slipping back into the negative feelings for "Bill." However, as you continue this practice of interrupt and substitution, you'll discover a shift in the energy you feel for "Bill." Eventually, you'll no longer experience a negative charge when you think of "Bill." As you continue the practice, you'll even begin to experience more positive, compassionate feelings toward the individual you were upset with.

When It's A Situation or Condition:

As with the forgiveness practice for individuals, bring to mind the situation or condition that caused upset in your life or the life of someone you care about. It might be the economy, a blizzard, or a fire that has stressed you. Notice the negative feelings that arise.

Next, bring to mind a situation or condition that brings you joy. It might be watching a sunset, reading a good book, or listening to classical music. Notice the higher-vibration feelings associated with this memory.

The Interrupt/Substitute Practice: Follow the same process described under "When It's People." When you think of the stressful situation or condition, interrupt the thoughts and substitute the image and feelings of that which brings you joy. Through this practice, whether for individuals or for situations and conditions, you'll notice a transformation.

EXERCISE 3

Bring to mind the person toward whom you're holding unforgiving, angry, resentful, or hurtful feelings. Say aloud:

"I forgive you for everything and anything you have said and done – past, present, and future. Please

forgive me for everything and anything I have said or done to you – past, present, and future."

"But I've done nothing that requires forgiveness," you might be thinking. You might not be aware of it, but there's probably something you have said or done (perhaps not directly), to that individual or situation, which has made you energetically part of the situation. We are all creators of our life experiences, so in essence, we are all responsible for what is happening in the world.

Simply holding onto the negative energy of unforgiveness invites the opportunity for forgiveness. Years ago I heard of a couple whose daughter was brutally raped and murdered. The man responsible was apprehended, convicted, and put in prison. The parents visited the man after his incarceration and asked for his forgiveness. Why would they ask for forgiveness? Weren't they the injured parties? Wasn't it their daughter who had been so brutally murdered? What could they have been thinking to visit their daughter's murderer and ask for forgiveness? The answer is simple. They realized the anger and resentment they'd been holding toward this man would negatively impact their own lives and the lives of everyone around them. For this, they asked forgiveness.

"Sacred Friends"

When asked how he could forgive the Chinese government for all the atrocities they had heaped upon the Tibetan people, the Dalai Lama responded that there were friends and there were "sacred friends." The Chinese government was his sacred friend.

Who's your sacred friend? What gifts has the person or condition you've forgiven contributed to enrich your life that you would not otherwise have received? How have you deepened your spiritual connection with your higher power? How have you been better equipped to serve others because of a stressful experience? What have you released because of your forgiveness process that opened your life to greater opportunities and good?

> *"Beneath the apparent circumstances of every situation exists a wholly different reality – a different world altogether."*
> – Colin Tipping

Chapter VII
ENERGIZE!

"Everything is energy and that's all there is to it. Match the frequency of the reality you want and you cannot help but get that reality. It can be no other way. This is physics."
– Attributed to Albert Einstein

"Your work is to discover your world and then with all your heart give yourself to it."
– Buddha

"Your material needs are provided as you follow your intuition and manifest your dreams into reality."
– Archangel Ariel

Celebrate!

This is a "STOP!" moment. This time, STOP and CELEBRATE!" You have taken the time to focus on the most important person in your life – YOU! How does that feel? Do you feel exhilaration? Joy? A sense of wonder? Anticipation? Love? Or do you feel uncomfortable? Selfish? Do you feel doubt? Fear? Now that you have named and declared your desires, are you starting to feel reluctant to continue on the path of your dream because you think you need to play small?

For many of you, this is new territory. You may be more comfortable focusing on the needs of others and putting their needs ahead of your own. If you are a caregiver, you may feel guilty when you think of putting yourself first. You might ask, "Who am I to think I could/should do this wonderful thing for myself?" My question is, "Who are you *not* to do this wonderful thing?"

In the movie *Coach Carter*, the coach keeps asking one of his players, Timo Cruz, "What is your deepest fear, Mr. Cruz?" The player doesn't understand the question, thinking he's just fine the way he is. It isn't until the end of the movie that Timo understands that he has been afraid – afraid of just how great he can be. He stands and speaks Marianne Williamson's powerful affirmation of worth.

Our deepest fear is not that we are inadequate. Our deepest fear is that we are powerful beyond measure. It is our light, not our darkness that most frightens us. We ask ourselves, Who am I to be brilliant, gorgeous, talented, fabulous? Actually, who are you not to be? You are a child of God. Your playing small does not serve the world. There is nothing enlightened about shrinking so that other people won't feel insecure around you. We are all meant to shine, as children do. We were born to make manifest the glory of God that is within us. It's not just in some of us; it's in everyone. And as we let our own light shine, we unconsciously give other people permission to do the same. As we are liberated from our own fear, our presence automatically liberates others.

– Marianne Williamson

Let your own light shine. Let it shine for yourself, if for no other reason than you are a demonstration of a magnificent, powerful Creator. Let it shine for others, so they can learn from your example and see that it is also their right to let their light shine. If you're a parent, this is your opportunity to model for your children, no nagging necessary. They'll see it in practice. If you're a business leader or supervisor, no disciplinary action required. Others will be inspired by your example. Being the greatness you truly are is not selfish. It is one of the most giving, caring things you can do – which means it's time for you to ENERGIZE this wonderful, powerful you!

Vibration

In the 1960s, the popular rock group the Beach Boys sang "I'm pickin' up good vibrations. She's giving me excitations. I'm pickin' up good vibrations." Then in the 1990s, Marky Mark recorded another "Good Vibrations" song with, "Come on come on. Feel it feel it. Feel the vibration. It's such a good vibration. It's such a sweet sensation."

One of the ways to energize your vision is to look at vibration – both of the vision itself and of you as you step into your dream.

Now that you've identified your purpose and passion, it's time to energize it and raise your vibration. Everything is energy. And everything has a vibration – the people you know, your pets, the animals grazing in the pastures, the plants, the trees, the chair you're sitting on, the waves in the ocean, even a boulder. Within everything are millions of subatomic particles bobbing and bouncing around. You experience vibration in every interaction. The clerk at the grocery store lifts your spirits with his high energy, while the woman in front of you in line drags you down because of her low vibration. You may not understand what's happening, but you know that at times you feel sluggish and at other times full of vitality. That's the power of vibration.

Why is creating and maintaining a high vibration essential to achieving your dream? It creates an attraction field that draws to you all the resources W. H. Murray promised. As the songs invite you, pick up the good vibrations, feel them, and savor the sweetness of high energy and positive sensations. We are magnets, always attracting and drawing to us people, resources, and experiences that are on the same vibration. I mentioned it in Chapter V under Gratitude. It's the law of attraction, and it's always at work.

That's why it's essential to develop and maintain a high vibratory level in your emotions and beliefs. In his book, *Power vs Force*, Dr. David R. Hawkins describes the energy levels of our primary emotions, ranging from the lowest vibration of shame, moving upward through guilt, apathy, grief, fear, desire, anger, pride, courage, neutrality, willingness, acceptance, reason, love, joy, peace, and enlightenment, the highest vibrational frequency level.

> *"If you wish to understand the Universe,*
> *think of energy, frequency and vibration."*
> – Nikola Tesla

I'm not asking you for enlightenment just yet – although that's the ultimate goal. I am inviting you to check in with yourself to see where you think you are now. Do you feel like you're vibrating at the level of the person who is already living your dream? If you are, fantastic! That means you are already attracting that life to you. If you are not yet at that level, you've got some work to do, and that's all right. Just the fact that you are becoming aware of different vibratory levels that attract according to their frequency is a huge step.

For now, I invite you to bring your vibration to the level of courage. Here you are stepping into self-empowerment, where you move from victim to victor, and where you recognize that you alone are in charge of your own life and have the power to choose how you respond to outside stimuli – where you step into living a possibility-led life versus a condition-constrained life. Through your vibration, you are the creator of your own world; and through your vibration, you change the world around you.

Lean Into Your Vision

You've written down your dream as if it has already happened. As if. This is an important step for living a life you love. Act *as if.* Act as if your dream has already happened. Become the person who has already achieved your dream. This includes thinking as if, speaking as if, and acting as if.

Remember my dream of traveling to Alaska? I initially chose that vision because I was inspired by the W. H. Murray quotation urging commitment. And yes, in some ways you might say I just made it up. Yet when I considered that vision, I saw that it had life for me. And what I mean by "life" is that it held energy, vitality, and excitement. I enjoy traveling. I enjoy being in nature. I enjoy new experiences. So I began to create the experience of Alaska.

First, I shared my vision with anyone who would listen to me. And because I was so clear and focused, others responded. My secretary ordered all the Alaska tourist bureau information she could get her hands on. A woman gave a presentation at my church about her year living in the Alaska wilderness. My friend's parents who lived in Anchorage, and whom I barely knew, offered to take me salmon fishing on the Kenai Peninsula when I got to town.

I decided I'd drive from Tucson, Arizona, where I lived, to the Arctic Circle north of Fairbanks, Alaska, and camp along the way. I went to just about all the auto dealerships in Tucson looking for the perfect vehicle for my trip. Even though his lot didn't have what I needed, the

Isuzu car salesman caught the vision and accompanied me to other dealerships to help me find the right and perfect automobile to take on my camping adventure.

What started out as something I made up because I thought it would be silly to leave my job without some sort of plan, came alive as I leaned into it. And as I leaned into my vision, my passion grew.

Be Passionate

Passion can be destructive or constructive. It is not neutral. Among the definitions in the Merriam-Webster dictionary are an "intense, driving, or overmastering feeling or conviction… an object of desire or deep interest." And that's the condition I'm inviting you into: be passionate! Passionate in a forward, positive, affirming direction. Passionate in a way that raises your vibration to the level of your vision, and of the person who is already experiencing that life. As you lean into your dream, you will notice this energizing, magnetizing passion growing in you. You will see new opportunities and resources that you might not otherwise have seen because you have opened yourself to possibilities rather than restricted yourself to conditions.

As I leaned into my vision, my excitement and passion grew. And I forged ahead with confidence and determination, even though I seemed to be taking actions out of any logical order. I sold my Toyota Corolla early in my planning stages months before I had decided on the best vehicle to take me to Alaska. But I got an immediate response to my ad at the price I was asking. So I had no car. I could call it luck that a friend was going out of the country for a month and didn't want her daughter driving her car while she was gone and loaned me hers. I could call it further luck that another friend had foot surgery when the first friend returned from her travels. And I could call it further luck that still one more friend bought a new car and was willing to loan me his old one.

But it wasn't luck at all. I had set a clear course, leaned into it, and fueled it with my passion. The Universe knew exactly what I needed and filled that need with three months of interim transportation until I decided to purchase a new GMC pickup truck and a used camper for my adventure. And in further support of my vision, when the Arizona Department of Motor Vehicles swooped in and confiscated all documents from the broker through whom I had purchased the truck, I was one of the few who had a clean bill of sale and was able to take possession of my vehicle.

It wasn't luck. It was simply clarity, creating a higher vibration, leaning in, and acting "as if" – all with a healthy dose of passion.

Celebrate Tiny Triumphs

I started this book by introducing Mattie, a stand-tall, courageous Arkansas woman who had a story to tell. I'll finish my own story later, but right now I'll take you back to Mattie. We had a lot of laughter during our coaching time together. The laughter came when I'd challenge Mattie on her stubborn "I've got to do it my way" approach to writing her book. First, she wanted to read Strunk and White's *Elements of Style* because her "I don't know how to write" and "I'm not educated enough" paradigms showed up from the start. Paradigm, in this case, is another name for mental mischief.

Mattie was up to something big, so she immediately found herself floundering in the doubts and uncertainties that rose up to drag her down. Her old paradigms tried to pull her back, eating away at her dream. For Mattie, even writing one page of her book was going to be a significant step.

We had our coaching call once a week, and each week we would set small, bite-size goals. At the beginning, we agreed to three handwritten pages per day, five days a week. "Is that something you believe you can do?" I would ask. "Yes, Ma'am," Mattie would reply. But we discovered three pages was too much. I asked, "How much did you get written, Mattie?" "I think I managed half a page each day," she'd respond. We celebrated the half page (tiny triumph), looked at what she saw about completing a half page versus three pages, and created new commitments that were a stretch for her, but which she could successfully meet.

Tiny triumphs. The new commitment was one handwritten page per day, five days a week. That, Mattie could do. Many outer circumstances were happening in Mattie's life. But one page per day toward the possibility of her completed book was something she could accomplish, even though it was a stretch for her at the beginning.

One page per day may not seem like much if you have a natural talent and proclivity toward writing. For Mattie, it laid the foundation for more "tiny triumphs" to celebrate, and it created an energy field of a higher vibration built on her small successes. She felt more confident as she leaned into her dream (acting "as if"). Her passion increased so that outer conditions didn't distract her, and she began attracting all the resources she needed to complete her book.

All this because we began with celebrating tiny triumphs.

Leaps of Faith

As you energize your vision, every now and then you must simply take a leap of faith. Faith, according to Merriam-Webster, includes a "firm belief in something for which there is no proof; complete trust." In Hebrews 11:1, faith is defined as "the assurance of things hoped for, the conviction of things not seen." "Hoped for" means you recognize it's possible. "Conviction of things not seen" recognizes that there's a higher power at work, an unlimited Universe yearning to express through you and fulfill your desires. There are times when it is faith that keeps us moving forward no matter what the outer conditions are.

You can have faith in the outer conditions and everything that can go wrong. You can have faith in "the evil eye" and curses. And you can have faith that when your medical doctor tells you you're going to die, you will die. Or you can have faith in possibilities – in having a direct connection with an abundant universe yearning to fulfill your every need and desire.

Possibility-based faith is that voice within you that overcomes debilitating mental mayhem, overpowers the doubters who surround you and vomit their fears and projections, and neutralizes the outer conditions that had prevented others from succeeding. "Possibility faith" makes you the person who does what "realistic" and "rational" people say is impossible.

You may have started this visioning process with little faith in the outcome, but possibility faith is what has grown within you like a mighty oak tree emerging from a tiny acorn – and in your case, the acorn is a dream for something greater than you ever imagined.

Possibility faith overcomes fear. When you move from the comfort zone of the familiar and known, it will feel either scary or anticipatory. If you feel fear, you might hesitate to move from the familiar toward your dream because it would take you into "terra incognita." If you feel a sense of anticipation and excitement, you are more likely to venture out even if you don't know "how."

Possibility faith raises your vibration so that you become courageous enough to step out of condition-based living into the unknown world of possibility and promise.

Chapter VIII

BRIDGING THE GAP

"The purpose of life for man is growth...Nothing that is possible in spirit is impossible in flesh and blood. Nothing that man can imagine is impossible of realization. Man is formed for growth, and he is under the necessity of growing. It is essential to his happiness that he should continuously advance."
– Wallace D. Wattles

From Where You Are to Where You Want to Be

There's the life you'd love and the life you're living. Sometimes I meet people who are already living the life they love. However, most people I speak to still have a yearning for something "more," even if they already have a comfortable life. And there are those who feel totally adrift with no hope of bridging the gap between the life they're living and the life they'd love.

If you've been doing the exercises in the earlier chapters of *Embracing Greatness*, you're getting in touch with the life you would love to live. Yet, there's still a gap between where you are and where your heart calls you.

I've already mentioned how much of my life was on autopilot, although on the surface it looked good. What I've come to realize is there were times I connected with a Greatness Success Formula that made it possible for me to achieve certain goals, regardless of outside conditions that said my dream wasn't possible, practical, or pertinent.

Looking back, I realize that the first demonstration of the success principle came in ninth grade, where I had been "tracked" for college-entrance classes. About halfway through the year, my mother told me we didn't have enough money to send me to a four-year college. My brother was in an undergraduate program, but he was living at home, and tuition and fees were low. I was to go through a two-year associate's degree program after high school, as my sister had, and study secretarial science. The cost would be about the same as my brother's bachelor's degree – even though the two-year program was a couple of hours away and involved dorm fees.

I generally did what my parents told me to do, so in tenth grade, I switched to secretarial practice classes even though I didn't want to be a secretary. My mother's belief was, "If you can type and take shorthand, you'll always be able to find a job." Because I had originally been college tracked, the school left me in the English, history, and other general courses with the college-entrance students. I kept taking German because my father and my mother's parents were from Germany, but I stopped math after finishing algebra in ninth grade and never picked up science.

I yearned for something other than "secretary" but didn't know what that might be. Mom's plan was simple: get a job, get married, have children, and stay home to raise them. None of that made my heart sing, yet I was going to follow "the plan" because that's just what one did. Plus, I felt a bit like a fish out of water with my fellow students in the college-entrance classes.

My father was an exterminator by trade. He may or may not have had the equivalent of our high school education (he immigrated to the United States when he was around seventeen years old), and didn't associate with the "yacht club" set, even though he owned his own successful small business. My college-entrance classes were filled with kids whose parents were professors or the "movers and groovers" in town.

Added to that was my father had begun drinking heavily when I entered high school. When he was drunk, he would tell me how stupid I was. And because of his alcohol-induced blackouts, he would regularly call me a liar when I did things he had given permission for. Let's just say my self-esteem was low. Plus I had always been a shy kid, so it never dawned on me I could strive to be anything other than what I was told I "should" be.

Yet I carried a discontent for something "more." However, I had no idea what that more was, and I felt too insecure to approach any of my teachers. By then I believed what my father said when he called me stupid; so I thought if I shared my desire to go to college, my teachers would laugh at me. The truth was that my college-track classes were honors classes, I had almost straight A's on my report cards, and I had been inducted into the National Honor Society. That's not to brag. It's simply to illustrate the disconnect we can have between our perceptions and limiting beliefs – and the truth of who we truly are.

Where are you experiencing a disconnect between your limiting beliefs and perceptions and the truth of how magnificent you are? Where are you allowing others' expectations to govern your life? And are you finally uncomfortable enough with the "same ol'" way of living that you're ready to leave behind "Old World" consciousness and venture out to the terra incognito of boundless possibility?

You're reading this book, and you've made it this far. If you've been doing the exercises, you're getting in touch with your dreams. So what are you going to do about it?

Are you ready to move forward and bridge the gap between where you are and where you want to be?

It's Your Time!

I was at a workshop where the leader shared actuarial tables of life expectancy on the screen. We were asked to find ourselves on the table and subtract our current age from our life expectancy. We were then to journal what we would do with the time between our current ages and projected dying. The exercise was pointless for me because I've witnessed so many people younger than I am who are already making, or have made, their transitions. It's not what we're going to do in the future that's important. It's "What am I thinking, saying, and doing in this moment?" and "Is what I'm thinking, saying, and doing bringing me closer to my dream?" Every moment is precious, and it's our job to make those moments worth savoring.

> *"...everyone wants to know that his or her life makes a difference – that we all count for something."*
> – Maria Nemeth, Ph.D.

This is your time! It's your time to create the life you love in every moment. So let's bridge the gap between where you are and the life you would love living.

The Greatness Success Formula

Throughout this book, I've presented the steps necessary to bring your dreams into physical reality. You know much of this intuitively. However, just as you need a form when you pour concrete to make a sidewalk, you also need a form to frame your dream. Otherwise, just as cement will spread in unintended directions if it doesn't have a frame, so will your attempts to create and live the life you love.

THE FORMULA

I = Inspiration *(The Inspired, Intuitive Idea)*
Anchored in S.M.A.R.T. Goals

+ P = Passion and Purpose

− B = Barriers *(Limiting Beliefs & Outer Conditions)*

+ A = Action

+ W = Willing to Receive

= S = SUCCESS *(Living the Life You Love)*

Remember my Alaska story in the Introduction and Chapter II? Without realizing it, I was following this Greatness Success Formula.

Inspiration

Inspiration often results from longing and discontent. In my Alaska experience, the inspiration came from a deep, painful discontent with my job. And pain is often the catalyst and inspiration to seek something different, something coherent with our Inner Truth. Ideas begin to percolate, and eventually, certain ones take on more energy than others. They evolve from "That's silly" to "Maybe I can."

Is pain necessary to experience inspiration and vibrant, exciting new ideas? No. I've met many people who are on a creative trajectory that is born of curiosity and an internal fire to ever evolve in all areas of their life. Like Phil, a man I know who has a loving family, thriving business, vibrant health, and the ability to do what he wants when he wants. I was attending an intensive offered by one of my mentors when I first met him. The seminar was aimed at creating happiness and abundance in all areas of your life. A lot of us attending were coaches and consultants. Phil wasn't.

After learning a little about his life, I asked why he was there. I was expecting an answer with at least a little frustration and discontent. Not at all, so I asked him, "Your life seems fulfilled already. Why are you investing your time and money to attend this event?" "I just thought it would be fun to try new areas of creativity," he responded.

In his case, it was to write children's books. He had already successfully published two. "It sounds like you're pretty self-directed and focused already. What prompted you to invest in this seminar?" I probed. "Well, coming here the first time gave me the confidence to try the crazy idea of writing children's books. It was so different from my professional life, I thought I was being silly," he said. "I'm here again to see what other 'silly' things I can do." In his case, he had a yearning to explore and create.

So if you think you need to be in pain for this formula to work, you don't. The truth is that it works for any creative endeavor.

In the case of my Alaska experience, my inspiration came from both my discontent and my love of travel and adventure. To make that dream a reality, I created a S.M.A.R.T. goal as an anchor and guide. If you've worked in administration or project management, you're probably familiar with this concept.

S.M.A.R.T. stands for Specific, Measurable, Achievable, Relevant, and Time-Based.

Specific:

The goal must be clear and unambiguous. If it's vague or too general, you'll have difficulty attracting the resources and support you need. Your energy and focus will be scattered. There will be too much room for confusion and uncertainty. And mental mischief will have far too much leeway to insert itself and undermine your realizing your dream. To help with specificity, you'll want to answer the basic five "W" questions:

- What do you want to accomplish?
- Why are you embarking on this journey?
- Who do you want on your team, who do you want to support you, who would you love to share this adventure with?
- Where will this happen?
- Which resources and requirements apply?

Measurable:

How will you know you've achieved your goal? How do you know how far you've come and how far you still need to go? How can you tell if you're off course? Some questions to answer include: How much? How many? Where?

Having a measurable goal gives you valuable feedback regarding if and when you need to make a course correction. It also gives you milestones for celebrating your progress and accomplishments. This provides the exhilaration of achievement that inspires and motivates you to continue your journey. Having a measure also tells you when you've reached your goal. What you measure grows. It sends a message to your subconscious that you're serious.

Achievable:

A goal should be within your capacity to believe you can achieve it, while still being a stretch. You don't need to know "how" – just "what." The "how" will be revealed to you when your goals are based on your dreams and inner urgings. You'll recognize new and creative ways to achieve your stretch goal. You'll develop the attitudes, abilities, skills, and financial capacity to reach them. To be a stretch is a personal measure. Remember, if reaching your goal is easy, it's not a stretch. Challenge yourself. If you can dream it, it means you have a deep inner belief you can achieve it. And if you commit to it, "Providence moves … A whole stream of events issues from the decision, raising in one's favour all manner of unforeseen incidents and meetings and material assistance…"

Relevant:

The goal must be relevant to your dream. If your dream is to own your own catering business, a goal of running five half marathons in the next six months, while admirable, isn't relevant to your goal and won't attract the types of human, material, emotional, and financial resources and support you need. If the goal isn't relevant to your dream, it will become a distraction and obstacle to achieving your dream. Having a relevant goal increases your passion and commitment to bringing your vision into physical reality. Ask yourself, "Is this goal worthwhile? Is it coherent with my Inner Truth? Will it take me in the direction of my dream?"

Time-Based:

A S.M.A.R.T. goal has target dates and times. Committing to a completion date or time makes setting priorities easier, helps you stay focused, and prevents unrelated interests or "urgent-but-not-essential" distractions from overtaking your day-to-day activities. Having time-based goals also creates a sense of urgency and allows you to set interim objectives and target dates. It also helps you answer the question, "What can I do in five minutes that will bring me closer to my goal?"

Did my Alaska trip fulfill this first part of the formula? Definitely. In the movie *South Pacific*, Bloody Mary sings, "You gotta have a dream. If you don't have a dream, how you gonna have a dream come true?" I had the dream:

experience Alaska and share the grand adventure with my mother.

And I fulfilled each of the S.M.A.R.T. goal criteria. My dream was to experience Alaska. The goal of reaching the Arctic Circle where it crossed the oil pipeline haul road north of Fairbanks was Specific. It was Measurable. I'd either be standing at the Arctic Circle or I wouldn't. It was Achievable, yet a stretch. It was about 11,000 miles round trip from Tucson to the Arctic Circle, and it was a camping trip – not your usual outing. The goal was Relevant to my Inner Truth of being an adventurer, experiencing beauty and new places, and being a loving daughter. And it was Time based. I knew I wanted to be back in Tucson by Labor Day because my mother had purchased her return airline ticket for that day. Interim, Time-based and Measurable objectives were based on the final date. I knew I needed to be in Prince Rupert, British Columbia, by a certain date to catch the inland ferry to Skagway, Alaska. I needed to reach the Arctic Circle by a certain date so I would have time to drive the 6,000 miles home.

Purpose and Passion

Purpose takes root in, and emerges from, your inspiration. Passion is the energy and emotion that gives you the drive, courage, and conviction needed to take your Inspiration from the visionary realm, where inspiration resides, into physical reality.

Why is it important to demonstrate your dream in the "relative world" of the physical senses? Have you ever met someone who says they're an author, that they have a "book within them"? How do you know it's true? Can you see what they've written? Feel it? If someone says they're a great singer, how do you know it's true if you've never heard them sing? How do you know someone is a great cook if you've never smelled or tasted something they've created?

Purpose and Passion take you from creative thought to creative expression. Mom and I reached the Arctic Circle, not just because I was inspired to make the journey. I could have visualized and meditated about the trip for months or years. But without the energy and urgency to actually embark on the adventure, I might still be sitting in my Tucson townhome dreaming about it.

Another reason Purpose and Passion are essential is that they raise your vibration to attract and match all the resources you need to bring your dream and the life you love into being. I was amazed how many people came forward to help me. Some of them were in my life briefly, but they played essential roles in clearing the way so I would reach my dream. Looking back, I'm not surprised. I shared my dream with anyone who would listen. The months of preparation for my trip were as exciting and fulfilling as the actual trip. I had fun, and so did everyone around me. It was contagious.

Purpose and Passion also fuel your commitment and drive to achieving your dream. When you wake up in the morning, you're filled with a feeling of excitement and expectancy, or an inner peace and a sense of knowing that you're being guided by a higher intelligence.

Eliminate Barriers

You must be willing to remove or overcome Barriers that stand between you and the life you would love. That might seem obvious, yet many people turn back when faced with challenges. Barriers can be internal, such as limiting self-talk, fears, and worries. And barriers can be external – people who doubt or try to block you, the economy, lack of resources, a physical or mental challenge, societal roles or expectations. The list is endless. However, you have a choice. Will you allow your internal mental mischief or external conditions defeat you? Or will you choose to be victorious as you follow the powerful pull of your dreams?

How can you eliminate barriers? Many of them will fall away simply because you've followed the first steps of the Greatness Success Formula. Your clarity, purpose, and passion – derived from the strength and focus of your inspiration – will help you break through internal barriers of self-doubt, fear, and feelings of insecurity. They will draw to you the necessary resources to overcome external challenges such as subterfuge from others or conditions such as a depressed economy, illness, death, natural disasters, or failed equipment.

There are countless "things" that can go wrong. However, every barrier will dissipate or you will find another, better path because of your higher consciousness and vibration. In every challenge, you will find a gift. You may learn new tools that help you achieve and maintain the life you love, make new relationships, gain deeper understanding, or recognize opportunities that you would not otherwise have seen. You will also eliminate and overcome barriers by taking Action, as described below.

For my Alaska adventure, I purchased a new three-quarter-ton GMC pickup truck to carry the fully self-contained camper I had purchased for the trip. The broker through whom I purchased the truck went bankrupt right after I gave him the money. Arizona Department of Motor Vehicles swooped in and confiscated all titles and documents of sale (Obstacle). Fortunately, the money I paid the broker made it to the dealership of origin just before the bankruptcy. However, the DMV didn't want to issue my plates until their investigation was over. That meant no Alaska trip (Barrier). However, my guardian angel, in the form of a very special DMV clerk, issued me a temporary registration and documentation so I could take my truck across the U.S.-Canadian border (Barrier dissolved).

Action

"And the day came when the risk to remain tight in a bud was more painful than the risk it took to blossom."
– Anais Nin

You must take Action! Too many dreams go unfulfilled because people get caught up in the dream without ever anchoring it in a goal, or they aren't passionate enough about bringing their inspiration into physical reality, or they succumb to the barriers that arise.

Action includes using your mental and physical muscles. This is an essential step because dreaming without action is just wishful thinking. And wallowing in discontent and yearning will just give you ulcers, dysfunctional relationships, addictions, an unfulfilled life, and general malaise.

Action with your mental and emotional muscles entails doing the internal work necessary to create the life you love. For example, strengthen your internal belief, faith, and resolve by daring to dream, then by anchoring your dream in your cellular memory by creating your life statement AS IF it has already happened. Remember the letter I was required to write, dated eighteen months in the future? It planted a seed in my cells so that as opportunities arose, subconsciously I "remembered" that this was the life I was meant to live. Those seeds grew into inspiration, determination, possibility faith, and decisions that created the life I love.

Internal work also includes prayer, meditation, and affirmations. When you're demonstrating the life you love, you need help from a higher/inner power greater than yourself. Through prayer, you name your desires. Meditation is how you can receive inspiration, guidance, and strength to claim your vision. Affirmations (positive statements affirming your dream "as if" it has already happened) are a powerful way to proclaim your dream. Name it. Claim it. Proclaim it.

Action is also putting feet on your dream – making the calls, signing up for the classes, taking the exam, writing the letters, looking for your dream home with a real estate agent, taking pen to paper (or fingers to keyboard) and putting the words down on paper that will become your book, doing what makes you uncomfortable, or jumping off the cliff (I mean that more as a metaphor, but you get the point). It's not enough to believe you can. You must take the physical action. This tells the Universe that you're serious.

To get to Alaska, I didn't sit around my townhouse waiting for Providence to knock on my door. I stepped out in possibility-based faith and took the actions in physical reality that needed to be taken as they revealed themselves to me. My moving forward in this way created an open pathway for Providence to rush to me "all manner of unforeseen incidents and meetings, and material assistance."

Remember Goethe's couplet: "Whatever you can do, or dream you can, begin it. Boldness has genius, power and magic in it."

Be Willing to Receive

I'm still in awe, but no longer surprised, by how many people stepped forward to help me achieve my Alaska dream and how many unexpected blessings showered upon me. The people who helped became part of my dream. I tend to be independent and think I need to do most things on my own. But I never would have made it to the Arctic Circle if I hadn't been open and willing to receive the support and assistance of others – as well as the inspiration, insights, and guidance from God.

All the resources and support you need to create the life you love are waiting for you. All you have to do is be willing to receive. The cartoon character Pogo said, "We have met the enemy, and he is us." Don't be your own enemy. Become your own best friend by loving yourself and seeing yourself worthy enough to receive the vast and unlimited abundance of the Universe.

Success

What is success? The Merriam-Webster dictionary defines success as: "the fact of getting or achieving wealth, respect, or fame; the correct or desired result of an attempt." Dr. Maria Nemeth, founder of the Academy for Coaching Excellence, defines it as "doing what you said you would do with clarity, focus, ease, and grace." Poet and author Maya Angelou says "Success is liking yourself, liking what you do, and liking how you do it." And Wallace D. Wattles wrote that "...success is attainment, without regard to the things attained. ...the cause of success must be in the individual." I say, "Success is living the life you love." What's your definition?

The Mr. Young Difference

I began this chapter with the story of wanting to go to college but being told we couldn't afford a four-year university. Not only did I go to the State University of New York at Albany straight from high school, five years after I graduated with my Bachelor's degree, I attended Cornell University and later received a Master's degree in Industrial and Labor Relations.

What changed? Did our financial circumstances change? No. Did some mysterious benefactor show up at our door with the money? No. Did I receive a full scholarship? No. What happened? Mr. Young happened. Mr. Young was my high school guidance counselor. When I was in the eleventh grade, Mr. Young asked me if I had ever thought of going to college. Forgetting that I was "stupid," I said, "Yes, but my parents told me we don't have enough money." To this day I have no idea what Mr. Young's first name was, but he changed my life – both by his question, "Have you ever thought about going to college?" and his response when I told him we didn't have the money. "The State of New York offers college loans. I think you'd be eligible."

My discontent and yearning had been heard even though I never said a word. Filled with hope, I went home and told my father I wanted to go to college. He responded, "We don't have the money. You have to go to a two-year school, like your sister." "But Mr. Young says we can get a student loan from the State of New York," I said. My father only grunted and looked away. I figured that was it. No university for me. However, Mr. Young had given me the validation and support I yearned for, and I had planted the seed of my dream (Inspiration/Idea) by speaking with my father. When Dad came home from work the next evening, he told me he had looked into student loans, and I could go to a four-year college.

That's when purpose and passion kicked in. Although most universities required four years of high school math and at least two years of science, I had at least fulfilled the foreign language and grade point average requirements. I discovered that two New York State Universities would accept my secretarial practice classes in lieu of science if I applied for business teacher training. All I needed was to take tenth-grade plane geometry. So in my senior year, I sat with sophomores, who thought I had flunked the class twice and was there in a last-ditch effort to pass. I didn't care. I had overcome the barriers of "not enough money" and "not enough science and math."

I applied and was accepted to Albany State University. Three and a half years later, I graduated with my Bachelor's degree in English Education (I had changed my major as soon as I entered college). My father died soon after, and I moved back home so my mother wouldn't be alone. I discovered that there weren't any teaching jobs in Ithaca. All that I could find was Senior Administrative Secretary at Cornell University. (What was that about not wanting to be a secretary?)

After working my way up to higher-level administrative positions over the next five years at Cornell, I hit a wall. As I applied for management positions, I was told I couldn't have the higher-level jobs because I didn't have a Master's degree. This was during the Women's Liberation Movement. Although I had no proof, I believed I was facing sex discrimination and thought, "Two can play this game. I'll just get my Master's degree."

Here's where the Formula for Success really kicked into high gear.

Inspiration:

My Inspired Idea was clear: Master's degree. I made my decision early in the year and set about finding a major that I would enjoy and had good prospects of professional employment when I graduated. After reviewing the many programs at Cornell, I decided on the School of Industrial and Labor Relations. My S.M.A.R.T. goals were easy. Specific: Master's Degree. Measurable: I'd know when I had it. Achievable: I never doubted I could do it. Relevant: I wanted to grow professionally. Time-Based: I would begin school in September of the same year.

Passion and Purpose:

I made the decision to attend graduate school in early spring with the full intention of starting the same fall. I hadn't even taken the graduate record examinations (GRE), yet I never doubted that Cornell would accept me. So in March, I went to my boss and announced, "Irving, I just want you to know that I'll be leaving in August so I can attend graduate school this fall." Irving was a little surprised, "That's great. But I didn't realize you'd even applied." I explained that I hadn't, but I would be taking the GREs that month and would apply as soon as I had my results. Irving gave me a quizzical look, but only said, "I'll miss you." I could tell he doubted that I'd be leaving that year because he knew the "rules" – you had to apply to college a year in advance.

Barriers:

The main barriers I faced were an average grade point average from undergraduate school, an average score on my GREs, and applying only a few months prior to when I wanted to enter. That might not have been a big deal somewhere else. However, I was applying to one of the best industrial and labor relations schools in the country at an Ivy League university.

Action:

But I was so clear and definite in my purpose, I discounted the "rules" (aka outer conditions). I took the GREs in March, received my results in mid-April, immediately submitted my application for that September, and was accepted in May.

Willing to Receive:

Throughout this process, I assumed my Inspiration would become reality, and I was willing to receive. And because I had been so plugged into the power of the Greatness Success Formula, I attracted even more good in the form of a full fellowship, which I was offered by the first week of June.

Success:

I did it. There were some hiccups and distractions along the way; but throughout my journey, following the Greatness Success Formula brought me to the achievement of my dream – receiving a master's degree.

She Bridged the Gap

I've shared these stories from my life so that you can see why I *know* these principles work. This isn't theory. I've seen these principles work over and over and over again.

Roberta

Early in my health-care career I met Roberta, a remarkable woman who was a shining example of using the Greatness Success Formula to bridge the gap between the life she was supposed to live and the life she hungered for. Roberta was hired to help set up a new department at the hospital where I worked in administration. I was impressed by her calm, heart-centered approach to everything she did. She identified what needed to be completed, created the team and found the resources necessary to accomplish her department's goals, and was a consummate student and teacher. Over the years we worked together at the hospital, she and I forged a friendship that has lasted several decades.

The Roberta I initially met was a successful professional and mother. She went on to serve in the state legislature and work as an influencer and liaison in state government. Although now retired, she is still a highly respected member of her community. As I got to know Roberta, I learned of her humble beginnings, her lifetime of overcoming adversity, and her continuous evolvement and growth.

Roberta was raised by her grandparents, who did their best to give her a good home, even though they didn't have much money. Roberta had a dream of becoming a nurse. Her grandparents couldn't support that dream on several fronts. First was not being able to provide the transportation to the city where entrance exams were held. Second was the lack of money to pay for nursing school, even if she was able to take the exam and be accepted. And third was that becoming a nurse was outside what her grandparents thought was possible for someone in their circumstances.

Roberta's "Mr. Young" was Mrs. Johnson, the mother of a classmate. Roberta still remembers Mrs. Johnson sitting on the couch in her grandparents' living room, so short that her feet didn't touch the floor. Mrs. Johnson was driving her daughter to take the nursing school exam and offered to take Roberta. At first, Roberta's grandparents resisted because there would be no money for school even if Roberta passed the exam. But, in the end, they relented.

Roberta's Inspiration was clear – she wanted a better life, a life filled with promise and purpose as a nurse. It was anchored in a S.M.A.R.T. goal – becoming a nurse. And she was Passionate. It was the energy and vibration of her passion that attracted all the resources she needed to overcome the Barriers of financial lack and expectations of what she "should" do because of the conditions of her outer circumstances. She attracted Mrs. Johnson to provide the needed transportation. Once she passed the nursing school entrance exam, she attracted the scholarship funding to complete the program.

Roberta got married, had children, divorced, raised her children as a single mother, grew professionally, and was elected to state office. Throughout her life, Roberta continued to grow in emotional well-being, spiritual unfoldment, professional achievement, and service to her community. She could easily have accepted the outer conditions of her early years and lived a condition-based existence. Instead, she chose a possibility-led and inspired life.

Bridging Your Gap

I could fill volumes with Greatness Success Formula stories like Roberta's. She is just one of the incredible people I've been privileged to meet over the years. I'm excited that I get to meet *you* through this book. Even though we haven't yet met in person, I know how amazing you are. I see the greatness that resides within you, yearning to be demonstrated in the world.

I'm excited for you. You have a desire in your soul that shows up as an idea, an inspiration, or a "what if?" thought. You might not yet have identified and acknowledged the life you'd love to live. But it's there, ready and waiting to be uncovered.

What's your Inspiration (your Inspired, Intuitive Idea)? Do you want to be in a loving, committed, supportive relationship? Do you want to travel the globe? Do you want to cater unique specialty desserts? Do you want to be CEO of a Fortune 100 organization? Do you want to retire from your "day job" and have fun, profitable side activities? The Inspiration is in you.

I recently met Joyce, a woman in her early thirties who is two credits short of a bachelor's degree, has served in the United States Navy, and is now searching for "what's next." I asked her, "What would you love?" She responded,

"I'm so scattered, I have no idea – and that's what's so frustrating." So I rephrased the question, "What would you love if you didn't believe it was impossible, impractical, or irrational?"

By inviting her to step away from condition-based thinking and enter the realm of possibility-led inspiration, she was able to connect with a yearning that she hadn't allowed herself to acknowledge. "I'd like to go to Argentina and Chile. Then I'd like to see Ireland and Scotland. Oh, and France and Spain. And..." As Joyce paused for a breath, I said, "So you want to travel the world?" Joyce paused for a moment and said, "Yes, but I don't want to have to pay for it." I laughed and said, "Sounds like you do have a dream – you'd like to travel the world on other people's money. Right?" She nodded. "See what you can get in touch with when you set aside what you think is rational or practical or fits what other people think you should do?" I asked. Joyce laughed, and acknowledged that our conversation gave her a new sense of hope and purpose.

Does Joyce's dream seem extravagant or impossible because of her circumstances? If you say yes, I invite you to look beyond outer conditions. I can think of many possibilities that would make Joyce's dream come true. It's Joyce's decision whether or not to follow her dream. If she does, I'm confident she'll be able to raise her vibration to attract all the resources (ideas, people, finances, opportunities, etc.) needed to live the life she would love.

How about you? What would you love? What's your Inspiration – your Inspired, Intuitive Idea? Are you ready to put the Greatness Success Formula to work in your life?

Chapter IX

EMBRACING GREATNESS:
YOUR TOOL CHEST

*"Some people don't like you because
your strength reminds them of their weakness.
Don't let their hate slow you down."*
– Thema Davis

*"You don't have to take everything so seriously. Life isn't
black and white, answers aren't always yes or no, and
absolutely nothing has to happen today. Act when you're
ready. Be led by your feelings. And the next time someone
wants to fit you into a mold, just tell 'em that your jeans are
in the wash, your angels are at the mall, and Oprah's on
the other line.*

*Fuzzy as dice,
The Universe*

*P.S.: You're a spiritual being, on an eternal quest in a love-
adventure you get to design. Do it your way."*
(from "Notes from the Universe"
by Mike Dooley www.tut.com)

Have you ever considered what you would need if you were ever stranded on a remote island with no hope of rescue? Sometimes I'll joke with friends that if I were in that situation, a library would be at the top of my list. The second thing I'd want is a hardware store or a good old fashioned general store that had a little bit of everything. I enjoy wandering the aisles of hardware and general stores. They carry such a fascinating array of goods, among them tools. The interesting thing about tools is I like to have them at my disposal in case I need one, even if I don't know exactly how to use it. But that's what the library's for – to show me how to use the tools.

Consider this: the Earth we live on is that deserted island. The library is all the information and wisdom you need to live an abundant, joyful, and prosperous life filled with love, adventure, vibrant health, peace, excitement, promise, and possibilities beyond your wildest imagination. The hardware store has all the tools you need to bring your dreams of a life you would love into full reality.

And you already have access to all that you will ever need to live the life you would love! If you've been doing the exercises in this book, you're already seeing positive results. This chapter is part review and part added tools.

Name It. Claim It. Proclaim It!

In order to achieve what you want in life, you must first name it. If you want apple pie with vanilla ice cream, first you must identify it as your desire. Otherwise, you might end up with a strawberry torte drizzled with chocolate syrup. Many of the exercises in this book are an invitation to name (identify) what you desire as the magnificent, creative being you truly are.

I asked you to claim your desires and dreams by writing them down and expanding on what your life looks like when you're living the life you would love. You anchor and claim your dream when you write it down. It's there to reflect on, to deepen, and to embrace more fully. Writing tells the Universe/God/Higher Power and your own higher consciousness and subconscious that you're serious.

And you must proclaim the life you would love by taking action. Action might be something as simple as making a phone call or attending an event where you will meet people and find resources that bring you closer to your goal. Action includes doing the exercises in this book, hiring a coach, reading books and articles that support your dream, creating and repeating affirmations in alignment with your goals, or meditating.

It's your dream – not mine, not your partner's, not your parents', not your employer's, and not society's. It's *your* dream. Name it. Claim it. Proclaim it!

What Would You Love?

> *"Follow your bliss and the world will open*
> *doors where there were only walls."*
> – Joseph Campbell

What would you love? I've asked you this many times throughout *Embracing Greatness: A Guide for Living the Life You Love.* I'm taking you back to that question now and ask that you answer it again. If it's apple pie with vanilla ice cream that you want, then own it by being truthful – first to yourself. Essential to living the life you would love is allowing yourself to identify what that looks like. To review:

Consider your

- Relationships
- Career/Vocation/Creative Expression
- Financial Well-being
- Physical Vitality/Health

- Ability to do what you want, when you want, where you want, and with whom you want

In each area,

- What is your discontent, what are your yearnings?
- If you didn't believe it was impossible, irrational, illogical, or unreasonable, what would you love?

If you could have what you would love, what would your life look like in three years? In two years? In one year?

What S.M.A.R.T. goals can you create to anchor each area?

What barriers stand between you and where you want to be in each area?

Are you experiencing any anger, resentment, frustration, or other negative emotions that are holding you back from realizing your dream? Are you ready to release the barriers that these negative emotions have created?

This is the beginning. Take these creative ideas and drill down to give them life. Call on your five senses (sight, smell, hearing, touch, and taste) as you describe what you would love in each area. This is your creation. This is your life. This is your opportunity to infuse your whole being – your thoughts, emotions, spirit – with a calm assurance that you're already living the life you would love.

Staying On Purpose

It's easy to get waylaid when you're on your way to living the life you would love. It's called "distraction." Distractions come in many forms.

- Self-doubt and fear
- Addictions (substance abuse, television, video games, Facebook, etc.)
- Activities that may be fun but are not related to achieving your goals
- Outer conditions that make it appear you'll never succeed
- Health challenges
- Putting others' needs before your own
- Confusion

The list is long, and I've covered many of the distractions in earlier chapters. You've just spent time identifying what you would love in the areas of Relationships; Career, Vocation, Creative Expression; Financial Well-being; Physical Vitality and Health; and the Ability to do what you want, when you want, where you want, and with whom you want.

You've begun creating S.M.A.R.T. goals and identifying barriers that might stand in your way. It's time to infuse your desires with the power of your mind.

Affirmations

Affirmations are how you infuse your belief system with the knowingness and confidence that what you seek has already occurred. The saying, "Thoughts held in mind produce after their kind" is true. Affirmations help anchor confident, constructive thoughts so they become magnets for the good you want to see in your life. To affirm a thing is to positively establish that it is so, even (or especially) in the face of opposite and contradictory evidence.

When you use affirmations, you are programming your subconscious to believe that what you desire is already yours. Therefore, your affirmation is always stated in the present tense. It states what you want, NOT what you don't want. To say, "I don't want to be poor" sends out a vibration at the level of "poor." Your subconscious doesn't hear the "not." It only hears "poor."

I was once coaching an executive who was upset with the board of directors at her company. I asked, "What do you want in a board?" She responded with a litany of what she didn't want. "I don't want them to interfere with how I operationalize the company's vision. I don't want them to undermine my authority with the executive staff and employees. I don't want them to…." I stopped her before she got too far with her "don't" list with a simple question. "What *do* you want?" She had difficulty identifying and expressing what positive, supportive attributes she wanted to see in her board. So we worked on reframing her "don't wants" into a higher-vibration, positive *"do want"* list. Only then could she create her supporting affirmations.

What do *you* want?

Do you want a loving, supportive, exciting romantic relationship? Your affirmation might be,

> *"I am a magnet for a loving, joyful, gentle man/woman who is supportive, prosperous, and healthy."*

Do you want financial and professional abundance? Your affirmation could be,

> *"I easily create financial wealth while doing what I love and serving others."*

If health is your focus, affirm,

> *"I am whole and healthy in mind, body, and spirit. My body is vibrant and physically fit."*

Do you want a thriving business? Create an affirmation to reflect your burning desire. For example,

My business thrives as it serves our customers, our employees, and our mission. We attract all the human and financial resources we need.

Whatever you desire, affirm through the power of the written and spoken word that it is already occurring. After you create your affirmations, making sure to write them down, refer to them throughout the day, especially upon arising and before retiring for the night. When you do this, you're programming your belief system to accept this new, higher-vibration reality as your own. Consistently referring to and saying your affirmations also helps you to stay on track for achieving your goals and living the life you would love. Distractions will lose their power to keep you from your good.

Meditation

Once thought to be "woo woo" and "New Age" and a practice confined to religion (especially Eastern religions), meditation is now accepted, practiced, and encouraged in the West among many mainstream businesses, support groups, mental-health practitioners, and as part of traditional medical healing practices.

Meditation can help you relax, heal, be more creative, increase your inner life force (qi, ki or prana, etc.), shift your consciousness, find answers and insights to challenges you may be experiencing; become forgiving, compassionate, and loving; enjoy life more fully; and experience a closer relationship with your Higher Power/God/Spirit/Source.

You've seen pictures of yogis and Eastern monks sitting in meditative positions. Google "meditation" and you'll find images of people sitting on the floor in lotus positions with legs crossed or seated in a chair, usually with a straight back, uncrossed legs, and hands with palms facing up or down. Some meditation techniques involve chanting, using prayer beads, clearing your mind, concentrating on a particular mantra, eyes closed, eyes slightly open and focused on a spot, or walking. Which technique is best for you? Try as many meditation approaches as you need to until you find the one that fits you best.

There are many books, workshops, and retreats on meditation. Actually, you probably already meditate, although you might not call it that. To get started, find a comfortable position and quietly turn your attention inward.

Breathe deeply, concentrating on your breath. Allow yourself to relax and become peaceful. You'll notice a shift in your energy – you'll feel calmer, more focused, more peaceful and at ease. Are you looking for the answer to a challenging situation? Ask for guidance while in this peaceful, meditative state.

You can meditate at the office, while standing in line, with your children running around you, or at a concert or sports event. You can meditate even in the midst of seeming chaos. Or go apart for a while, separating yourself from the distractions of family and business responsibilities, telephones, the Internet, television, etc. Go into nature or simply close your bedroom door.

Whatever your approach, remember, do what works for you. Meditation is about stepping away from distractions, connecting with your inner wisdom, and drawing from the unlimited guidance and resources you already have within you.

Your "What's Mine To Do?" List

You have within you all the inspiration and ideas you need to live the life you love. Too often, you hold yourself back by discarding ideas because they're impractical, impossible, silly, stupid, never been done before, etc. Before the idea even sees the light of day, you've already dismissed it – or you've allowed someone else or outer conditions to dismiss it.

But what if your ideas were possible? Would that be all right? What if you could sail around the world? What if you could fly? What if you could walk on the moon? What if you could run a mile in four minutes or less? What if you could live because someone else's heart is beating in your chest? What if? Everything I've listed here has happened, so now it's "What is." But once, each was a "What if?"

Your dream of living the life you love is your "What if?" Now that you've established and claimed it, you can ask yourself a "how" question such as "What can I do to achieve my dream?" And then you write down ideas as fast as you can, with no editing or judging of the value of the idea. I've seen this process called brainstorming, sourcing, discernment, and co-creating. All it means is that you ask a question and write down all the ideas that come to you as fast as you think of them. If you have a trusted friend or colleague, invite him or her to join you in sourcing ideas.

Two things to remember while creating your list are:

- Ask the right question. Physicist Werner Heisenberg said, "What we observe is not nature itself, but nature exposed to our method of questioning." The quality of your "What Can I Do? list is determined by the quality of the question you ask. You might ask, "If I didn't believe it was impossible, how could I fulfill my dream of owning my own business?" Or "If I didn't think it was impossible, how could I find my perfect mate?"

- Write down any and all ideas that come to you. You can go back and edit later. During the creative stage, no judgments are allowed.

Like-Minded People

If you want to be an eagle, fly with eagles; don't walk around in a chicken coop pecking in the dirt. Find other eagles and soar with them. There are many ways to find others who are already living your dream or are on a similar path.

If you're looking for a perfect mate, join organizations where the man or woman you're looking for is likely to be. Check if there's a Meetup.com group in your area. Ask your friends. Do you want to create a beautifully landscaped back yard by yourself but don't have the expertise? There's probably a garden club in your area. Also, nurseries and hardware stores have staff who can help you.

If you want to build a thriving business, find the people who have already built successful businesses. Check for chambers of commerce. In the United States, there are many, including the city or town you live in, the Hispanic chamber, the Philippine chamber, women's chamber, GLBTQ chamber, etc. Is there a professional organization you could join? Check the events and networking sections of your newspaper or specialty publications.

The Internet is a powerful resource to find groups and activities where you will meet like-minded people. If you're on a spiritual path, find a religious or spiritual organization you resonate with. Contact social service agencies, S.C.O.R.E. (Service Corps of Retired Executives), or Meetup.com. The list is endless. Just start asking around and you'll connect.

MasterMind

Along the same line as connecting with like-minded people is to form or join a MasterMind group with people who share the same values and dreams as you. I found my MasterMind group through my local chapter of the National Speakers Association. We have varying levels of expertise in our speaking, writing, and coaching fields. We complement each other, so where one member needs to develop an expertise, another member can help. We share our dreams and challenges, information on the projects we're working on, and the support and accountability that brings us individually and as a community closer to achieving our goals.

I have other MasterMind relationships that are sometimes project-specific or ongoing. In each, members grow and thrive according to the level of participation and commitment that each one invests. My MasterMind groups are free. There are many that you can pay to belong to that have leaders trained in how to guide and nurture business people. Whether or not there's a fee associated with the MasterMind, check out the character and competence of the group members and leaders. And remember, when you select your MasterMind group, look for eagles.

Acting "As If"

Whatever your dream, whatever the life you love looks like, begin thinking and acting "as if" it was already yours. As a guide, ask yourself,

- What would the person who is already living this life be thinking, saying, or doing right now?
- How would that person dress?

- Where would that person go?
- How would that person express herself or himself?
- How would that person "show up"?

Do you want a loving relationship? Ask yourself, "What would the person who is already in a loving, nurturing, supportive relationship be thinking, saying, or doing right now?" How would you dress? Where would you go? How would you express yourself? How can you "show up" so that you attract the man or woman of your dreams?

You might want to have a luxurious home and high-end automobile. What would you be thinking, saying, or doing? How about dressing like the person who already owns the house and car. Go to open houses for the type of home you desire. Take a photo of you standing outside the home. Test-drive the car of your dreams. Have the salesperson take a picture of you behind the wheel.

If it's a thriving business you envision, ask the same questions. Then do what your answers require you to do, continuously asking, "What step can I take in this moment to bring me closer to my dream?" If you have five minutes, ask, "What can I do in five minutes that brings me closer to my dream?" Every moment is a choice point. Choose the thoughts, words, and actions that bring you closer to your goal.

This is Your Life!

Thank you for joining me on this journey called "Life." My desire is that you have gotten in touch with your unique purpose and passion for your time on Earth. Life is a precious gift – one that we all too often take for granted.

> *"Whatever you can do, or dream you can,*
> *begin it. Boldness has genius,*
> *power and magic in it."*
> – Goethe

This is your life! What would you love? Capture your dream and bring it into physical reality. There are those who say that doing what you love is "selfish." Actually, doing what you love is the greatest service you can give – to yourself and to everyone around you. Love has one of the highest vibrations of all emotions.

As you raise your vibration to love, you raise the vibration of all. It begins with the ones with whom you are most intimate. They witness your growth and blossoming and are drawn to your higher vibration. They'll want some of what you have; and when they want it passionately enough, they'll do the work necessary to raise their own vibrations and live the life they love. Then those in their circles will see what they've accomplished and will want it for themselves.

It's like throwing a pebble into a still pond. There isn't just one ripple. The ripples (your impact) extend outward until they reach the shore. You are a powerful being. You have a greatness within you that yearns to become visible and demonstrate in the world.

This is your life. This is your time. Let your light shine as a beacon of promise and hope for others. Let your light shine to make this world a better place for all. And in all ways, remember to embrace your greatness!

To continue your journey to live the life you love and to receive free gifts and updates, go to www.EmbracingGreatness.com.

ACKNOWLEDGMENTS

There are so many people who have helped me along my path. Only a few of them are mentioned in this book. Of course my family, including Mom and Dad, brother Ernest Falke and sister Nancy Merolle, who were an integral part of my formative years and remain a loving presence in my life. I talked about the Mr. Young difference. The truth is everyone we encounter throughout our lives makes us who we are today. I think back to the influence of teachers, many of whom called me higher and taught me critical thinking.

My work mentors were many. Of special note is Alethea Caldwell Munsinger, who saw promise in me when I came out of graduate school. She widened my horizons, both literally when she moved me from upstate New York to Los Angeles, California, and figuratively when she recognized my creativity, ability, intelligence, and trustworthiness. Alethea hired me four times and introduced me to a career in healthcare administration.

My life was stretched and enriched by my amazing coaching instructors and mentors at The Academy for Coaching Excellence in Sacramento, California, where I received my first coaching certification. They include founder Dr. Maria Nemeth and faculty members Reverends Beth Ann Suggs and Wayne Manning. More recently, deep gratitude to Mary Morrissey, Kirsten Welles, John Boggs, Rich Boggs, Jennifer Jimenez, and Mat Boggs of the Life Mastery Institute. Felicia Searcy demonstrated what can be done, and Tiffany Largie showed me how. And to my first Unity ministers Rev. Richard Rogers and Larry and Mary Ellen Schwarz and the faculty and staff of Unity Institute, thank you! You helped open up a new world of Truth for me that led to my years of service as a Unity minister.

When I shared my desire to write this book, coach and entrepreneur Missy Day continuously encouraged me to tell my story and graciously agreed to review the final draft. I'm grateful to colleague and friend Herschella Horton for her counsel and content input. And many thanks to Las Vegas headliner Jeff Civillico, who likes to be known for Comedy, Juggling, Silliness, and Fun, and whose success story was an inspiration. Another inspiration was Terry Cole-Whittaker, who both demonstrates greatness and affirms it in others.

I'm grateful to Michelene K. Bell, owner/editor of the former *In Light Times* newspaper for the opportunity to write a monthly column for almost five years, keeping my writing muscles supple. Writing coach Denise Michaels helped with the construction phase of my book, and Tom

Bird supported me with parts of the writing and taking my book from initial draft to published work. Linda Lynch Johnson, Stacey Hall, and Jeff Bearden were part of my Master Mind group during much of the writing and gave me support. A shout out to Jana Stanfield whose song *I'm Not Lost. I Am Exploring* became my theme song during my year sabbatical from 2006 to 2007. I appreciate Kim D. Snyder, who has been a friend and personal guru over many cups of coffee over the years. And my thanks to colleague Kathleen Quinlan, MSW, LCSW, who reviewed the manuscript, and to Lisa M. Landis and Rev. Beth Williams for helping with final proofreading.

I found wonderful colleagues through local Toastmasters International groups and the Las Vegas chapter of the National Speakers Association (NSA). Thank you to Mike Rayburn CSP, CPAE for introducing me to NSA and your support of this book and to Darren LaCroix, CSP, and Ed Tate, CSP, for teaching me about business building in the public speaking industry.

I spent many hours writing at Pour Coffeehouse in Las Vegas and received warm support from baristas Emily Hahn and Sean Moore and owner barista Deborah Armstrong. Deborah reviewed a later version of *Embracing Greatness* from the perspective of someone who had opened a new business after working in a corporate job for many years. She gave me valuable feedback from the perspective of someone who, on her own, had already implemented many of the principles described in *Embracing Greatness*.

There are, of course, many more people I could mention. Each encounter in life – whether long-term or fleeting – makes a difference. To each of you who have guided and supported me along my journey, thank you! You have been a blessing, and I am grateful.

WHAT PEOPLE ARE SAYING ABOUT
EMBRACING GREATNESS

Sophia Falke has nailed it! In her own inimitable way Sophia helps you discover the beauty and purpose in your uniqueness, what you and YOU ALONE bring to and for the earth. It is fun, readable and totally applicable for all of us. Please read this book!

– **MIKE RAYBURN**, CSP, CPAE, Hall of
Fame Keynote Artist

If you're ready to live the life you would love, and willing to take the life-empowering steps toward your dream, then Embracing Greatness: A Guide for Living the Life You Love *is for you. You will forever thank yourself for reading and applying this wonderful book.*

– **MARY MORRISSEY**, International Speaker,
Best-Selling Author, CEO Consultant, Visionary,
Empowerment Specialist

"Embracing Greatness *is an exciting adventure for anyone who wants to discover and cast aside long-held barriers to personal success. Sophia Falke gives the reader practical tools designed to turn personal dreams into reality. I heartily recommend it as an invaluable resource for anyone determined to manifest their birthright to greatness."*

— **KATHLEEN QUINLAN**, MSW,
Licensed Clinical Social Worker,
Author/Producer of *The Land of Love.*

I remember the first time I met Sophia, she stood up to introduce herself and said, "In case no one has told you yet today, you are amazing." Wow! I thought. I was taken by her energy and power in that statement. I have the privilege now of calling her my friend. Her life is one of great wonder and achievements. But she would disagree saying, "It's just my life." The first time I heard the Alaska Story, I was moved to tears. How incredible to share such an experience with her Mom. In this book, you will be moved also. Sophia truly has a heart for others to help them embrace their greatness.

— **MISSY DAY,** Certified John C. Maxwell Trainer,
Speaker and Coach

As a business owner who left corporate life to start my own business, I was inspired by Sophia's message to never give up, never stop moving ahead a step at a time. One passage in Embracing Greatness that stood out to me from the book was when Sophia's dad, after telling her she could not go to college because of money, arrived home one evening and told her it was okay. This was a major change in her life. She did not question why he changed his mind. She did not hesitate. She signed up for college and began the next phase of her life. Sometimes it is not for us to question why, but for us to take advantage of opportunities. I live that every day in the coffee shop – why are some days slow and challenging and some days busy with a steady stream of customers in and out all day? Take advantage of the busy days and open your mind on the slow days.

– **DEBORAH ARMSTRONG,** Owner,
Pour Coffeehouse, Las Vegas, NV

Embracing Greatness is like taking a walk on a warm spring day with a much respected mentor while getting the pep-talk of a lifetime. Filled with inspiration, doable exercises, and heartwarming stories of real people making tremendous positive changes, this personal-growth handbook is a true gem!

– **CATE MONTANA,** MA, Author of *The E Word: Ego, Enlightenment & Other Essentials*